Ghost *of* Yesterday

POETRY BOOKS BY SUSAN TERRIS

The Homelessness of Self, 2011
Contrariwise, 2009
Natural Defenses, 2004
Fire Is Favorable to the Dreamer, 2003
Curved Space, 1998

CHAPBOOKS AND ARTIST'S BOOKS

Tale of the Doll & the Bootless Child, 2011
Bar None, 2010
The Wonder Bread Years, 2009
Chapbook on the Marketing of the Chapbook, 2009
Double-Edged, 2009
Buzzards of Time, 2008
Marriage License, 2007
Sonya, The Doll-Wife, 2007
Block Party, 2007
Poetic License, 2004
Susan Terris: Greatest Hits, 2000
Minnesota Fishing Report, 2000
Eye of the Holocaust, 1999
Angels of Bataan, 1999
Killing in the Comfort Zone, 1995

Ghost *of* Yesterday

NEW & SELECTED POEMS

SUSAN TERRIS

MARSH HAWK PRESS

East Rockaway, NY • 2012

ISBN-10: 0988235617
ISBN-13: 978-0-9882356-1-8

Marsh Hawk Press books are published by Poetry Mailing List, Inc.,
a not-for-profit corporation under section 501 (c) 3
United States Internal Revenue Code.

Front Cover:
Charles Burchfield, "Childhood's Garden," 1917. Opaque and transparent watercolor with
graphite on slightly textured cream-colored paper. Reproduced with the permission of the
Munson-Williams-Proctor Arts Institute, Museum of Art; Utica, NY.

Author Photo: Daniel Terris
Book design by Jeremy Thornton

Library of Congress Cataloging-in-Publication Data
Terris, Susan.
  [Poems. Selections]
  GHOST OF YESTERDAY : NEW & SELECTED POEMS / BY SUSAN TERRIS.
     pages cm.
  Includes bibliographical references and index.
  ISBN-13: 978-0-9882356-1-8 (alk. paper)
  ISBN-10: 0-9882356-1-7 (alk. paper)
  I. Title.
  PS3570.E6937G46 2013
  811'.54--dc23
                            2012047468

 Marsh Hawk Press
P.O. Box 206, East Rockaway, N.Y. 11518-0206
www.marshhawkpress.org

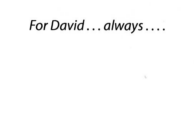

For David . . . always . . . .

Table of Contents

GHOST OF YESTERDAY: NEW POEMS

FIRE IS FAVORABLE TO THE DREAMER / 2003

CONTRARIWISE / 2008

THE HOMELESSNESS OF SELF / 2011

In & Out / Out & In

It's a pleasant thing to be young, and have ten toes.
—Robert Louis Stevenson

Oh how I love—not a fashionable statement now, much too sentimental an opening—*to go up in a swing.* No—wait—not that one but the *birdie with the yellow bill* who *hops.* Somehow, along with hop and cloy, there are images of an unspoiled world. Yes, I know them all—the ghost of yesterday, *shadow who goes in and out with me,* says how *we can be as happy as kings* (or queens) and that *rain* will go away. Or does he . . . .

Ghost *of* Yesterday

Ghost *of* Yesterday
NEW POEMS

Ghostlit

Major & Minor

When I get there, the lily is already wilting.
Then the ghost of yesterday tilts his head

And sits himself down at the piano.
If I were an old horse, he whispers,

I might have eaten the bulb that birthed
The lily. Instead, he places his long fingers

Upon the keys and begins to seesaw them
Through treble and bass, major and minor

Until the lily lifts her head, turns
Her pale face and gently pollens his chin.

Minor & Major

Please don't come, I tell my once-love, or
At last you'll know just how I feel.

The ghost of yesterday hovers behind me,
Pushing, nagging. Some mornings are easier

Than others, but today the snake is here, too,
Whispering in a minor key and wanting to

Know if it still hurts, that major space on
The left behind the lily of my breast, and if

Your familiar, the beast, comes at night to
Spoil illusion, to tweak the rib of loss.

Sink or Swim

Once at the lake was the summer of blood:
I was eight, had fish-eyes to see around

Corners as the doctor with the hairy mole
Put my mother on the white kitchen table

And took the not-quite baby away. The towels
Were wet-red. Then, while I danced alone in

A ring of mushrooms, they rocked my sister in
The toilet where she didn't know to swim.

Swim or Sink

Later, I pried chips from the rusty fungus
On the jack pine by the road, returned the crow's

Rasp, and picked goldenrod, which made Mother
Cry. The wash machine window showed pink

Bubbles, but I was a spider then weaving a web to
Wrap my sister. On the ends of her ten fingers,

I put salty Bugles, made her a sand castle,
And wondered if the water was clockwise or not.

Light & Dark

As always, the ghost of yesterday blows on
His black & white pinwheel when I want to

Forget the childhood mix of light and dark:
The girl cousin—blond, Siamese cat-eyed—

While I, dark scarecrow, was never favored.
Look at the photos from my dead father's Rollei:

See her curls/my black braids and unibrow.
My cousin's socks stayed up. She tattled; but I—

Unphased, baby existentialist, already *noir* — lit
Luckies for us on the woodpile by the garage.

Dark & Light

Complexity, like French braids and darkness,
I see now, is to be prized. Over time, my cousin

Dimmed, married a red-socked man; and she
Still remembers the Monday I stole her Monday

Panties and she, too mad to wear Tuesday, couldn't
Go to school. She may be lightning: sudden bursts;

But I, dark thunder, stay, collaborate and confuse.
Hey . . . the ghost prompts, *she does play bridge.*

I nod. Puppet girl, country club puppet woman.
Light hair, light head, a pale candle blown out.

Cock & Bull

No, not that kind of cock, but a fowl one who
Chased us when we collected eggs on

Susie's farm. At night, we'd lie on our backs
On the henhouse roof, suck just-picked plums,

Watch the Pleiades for shooting stars as we
Exchanged girlish bullshit of what we may or

May not have done with boys whose names we
Crosshatched on the raw edge of our books.

Bull & Cock

Bellow now. Use a mortar and pestle to make
A paste of days to rub in everywhere.

Mixed metaphor: but this is a rabbit-in-a-hat
Conundrum. If you don't pull it out, is it still there?

No more exchanges with girl-women—they
Can't keep secrets. Yes, bull and cock are literal

Now, preening and rutting. Life is experiential,
Existential. Always too secret to tender.

Rye & Ginger

Alas, but the ghost says I must confess, I
Had my first affair at 16. Though wearing

K's ID bracelet, I—nights when boys drank rye
and ginger—was playing chess with Topher.

Then, once, while K was on a booze-run,
Topher, by the pinball in our basement,

Electrified the angora of my sweater as we
Kissed and rubbed until K—

Returning—caught us. Topher, he yelled, is
Nothing! I will be *much* more successful!

Ginger & Wry

At our 25th school reunion, K—already
3 times married/divorced but an entrepreneur—

Introduced me to his new woman friend,
A ginger-haired nymph less than half his age.

Remember Topher, he said, smugly. Too bad
About the accident. Drunk, of course.

But—*you* are looking good. And, hey—your
Folks still have that pinball machine?

A real pinball, he told the gingersnap.
Bet I have 100 more free games still unplayed.

Claw & Tooth

It was the canoe trip where Frances hit the artery
In her ankle with an axe. After hours

Of direct pressure and dinner of burnt squaw corn,
The thirteen-year-olds woke me at midnight

Screaming, Bear! Bear in the campsite! Dazed yet
Oddly brave, I—counselor—stalked from my tent

With the blood-stained axe in hand to find
Only a hunched raccoon scarfing up garbage.

Tooth & Claw

When I was barely 18, parents trusted me with
Their children. Why? Whatever I did know has

Drifted off like milkweed silk. No more squaw corn:
politically incorrect. No more hatchets: too dangerous.

No counselors under 21, no open fires, no tenting near
Predators. And forget barbed hooks, canvas canoes

In white water. The wilderness has been Disneyfied.
But human nature remains red in tooth and claw.

Mind & Matter

At college, as I was moon-mad, trying to morph
From chrysalis to butterfly, two professors jumped

A stone wall as one—mine—said, Damn, speaking
Of *Wuthering Heights*, what a great book. Mine—

The campus Heathcliff—booked me for late notes in his
Basement office. As I stretched, he talked

Of (ghost is sawing a violin now) a Jewish Army buddy
And how many of his best friends, like me, were.

But the horned moon jabbed when I found he played
Vicky Gold the same tune. And Josie Mankiewitz.

Matter & Mind

Post-college, I never again saw the poet-professor.
But we wrote letters, phoned. O Duskywing,

he'd say seductively when he called. This is
Philip—the poet. Now I, in a tiny fox den of a cabin

Across from his home in Castine, stare at
Rocky shingle and lobster boats, and remember

His last letter to me: a high school football schedule,
A leaf, bookmark of a tumbling blocks quilt,

As he—deep in dementia—unable to phone, scrawled
His name on a paper napkin: Phillip with two l's.

Buck & Wing

When he braced his hands on my bare breasts,
I asked myself, Oh god, what have I done?

The white satin dress sat stiffly in the hotel
Chair rustling as I asked myself between bucks—

An unbuckled 21, buck naked, no bucks in the bank—
For the rest of my years, Who is he? Who am I?

Is this the scrapbook of a life or just scraps?
Is this eternity, or can I take wing and fly off?

Wing & Buck

Like a grounded raven, I pick my way over
An endless field of glacial scree. That white-dress

Dream was some other girl-woman.
Buck has slowed from gallop to trot to walk, and

I've lost the lyrics to the song of yesterday.
The children have morphed, as have I, yet not he.

He, my old love, once-love, is the broken wing
I drag, leaving a faint trail beside my dusty prints.

Write & Wrong

Hah! Two wrongs are still wrong, the ghost says,
Dragging me back to the graduate school seminar

Where we waited for my classmate to arrive,
One who said he was bringing his roommate to

Hear my paper. Classmate: a suave dude with
Aran sweater and Sherlock pipe who'd been sharing

His Snickers bars, flirting though he knew I was
Married. When he finally showed (*To be or not to be,*

The ghost snickers), dude had his right hand tucked into
His friend's back pocket. His roommate=his lover.

Wrong & Rite

Let's not talk about the elephant in the room. Some
People can't juggle wrong & rite, black or white.

But invisibility, when it comes, is a jolt. As it came to
The Stanford professor who said women students

Didn't see him any more. Ah, welcome to the Rite
Of the Three Wishes. Ask for a spouse, children,

Even a house: granted. But, as you age, don't waste
A wish on visibility. Think, instead (right? wrong?)

Of lifelines, timelines, and how easy it can be to
Transgress in a world where you are unseen.

Push & Pull

Illusion/allusion: the births pinwheel now
In my mind—the mirror babies and

The one where I sat and watched as I
Pushed her/him between splayed legs to see

A black-haired furred mammal, eyes wide,
Wrinkled bouquet of iron and flesh after the pull

Of crown, jut of elbows, how the nurses thought
I was 12, how there is no memory for pain.

Pull & Push

Surprise. It was indeed nature not nurture—
Pull-up, pull-toy, and push of bicycle but the self

Not to be mothered into any passages pre-set
Or predictable. Miracle of willful creatures,

Accident of core and cell, like Micawber's
Children, they tumbled up, pulling forward

Into a fogged future, full-formed, eyes ahead,
Not always grateful for a push from behind.

Oil & Water

When I peer down into the wishing well,
The mask of my face shivers up.

Though the oil-tarred bucket's full, my hands
Are empty. Percussion of the past drops

Stones that ripple, distort. The castaways,
The sand, the kites and cousins surface

As the ghost of yesterday dredges them up,
But glosses over the future. *It's all physics,*

He insists. Yes, oil and water may rainbow
But they separate and will not marry.

Water & Oil

Silhouettes pulse past me bearing spades
And buckets. Natural selection insists

That the girl who lied will always lie.
Earth's curvature and its spin persists; but

Emulsify is not my mantra. I'd rather stir
The past with one finger, find an oyster

Shell, dig for buried treasure, turn my back
On the slinking ghost. For me, an oily rainbow

In a bucket and two mutable faces are all that
Matter. Water the past but slick the future.

Flotsam & Jetsam

After Limantour Spit, we barbecue mussels
On Drake's Beach, fly the 30 foot dragon kite,

As the children roam, collecting treasure: a boot,
Bucket with a hole, a strand of knotted pearls.

Daughter, donning the pearls and a sea-grass crown,
Declares herself queen, so we build her a driftwood

Castle, circle it with the dragon and crowd in
Body to body. Flotsam, for this day, protected, safe.

Jetsam & Flotsam

Messages in bottles—we float them from Bolinas
Lagoon. Help . . . moonrakers have kidnapped us

At Duxbury Reef. Help . . . we are living the wrong
Lives. Where have the children gone? Can we go, too?

Discard. Discard everything. Throw all dead weight
Overboard. Lighten up. Don't look back.

Where are the life preservers to hold up our heads?
Is this life a life? Beware: here there be dragons.

Paper & Scissors

It's faded now, fading still—that fragile picture:
My mother, my father posed on a knobbed

Stump in an unknown river, eager, leaning
Away from undulation of water, from maple

And sumac. Two barefoot, confident, unknowing
Twenty-somethings. Butterfly effect—

Before the thread was scissored. Though the ghost
Of yesterday claps his hands, my parents keep

Escaping, while I, still unborn, a nesting doll,
Curl inside, hold brother, sister, and the not-to-be.

Scissors & Rock

Once there was an easy girl, a laughing woman,
Then an old woman who forgot the girl-woman

She used to be. Widowed years had hammered
Her rock-hard and insensible. The ghost offers up

A kaleidoscope of who she may have been,
The sharp shards of my father, too. But they click

From black & white to sienna to finger-cut red.
I batter the scope, scatter fragments. But unable to

Sort mother/ father, I know them not. Now I ask,
Having lost them . . . who am I then? Who?

Double or Nothing

It was a different era—my parents, like lovers
From Hummel greeting cards, cared more

For each other than for us. They smoked Luckies,
Drank bourbon on the rocks, golfed, bridged.

When my father died of cancer and another man
No-trumped into Mother's life, she said she wouldn't

Wash his socks, had made all the compromises
When married, and was not going to do that again.

Nothing or Double

As a hedge against time, Mother told us, be sure
To have more than one man in your life.

Did she? No way to know now. But I've tried out
Her theory—a kind of isosceles triangle with me

As the point. A precarious balance: marriage and
Shadow marriage, marrow and de facto marrow—

A doubling that doubles cores, gives nothing, leaves
Me poker-faced and still making all the compromises.

Cause & Effect

Because cumulous has swabbed the sky,
No constellations pinprick the dome of night.

Yesterday's ghost sits in the dark looking for
Fireflies that don't spark here any more.

He wants me to ponder the breast lost, then
Reconstructed, and the man who said flesh,

Even scarred, was good. Counterclockwise
Or in mirrors it looks soft, real. Good effect /

Sweet clause. I bargained here, thought I'd won.
Still, he looked and looked yet never touched.

Effect & Cause

The whitest lies and the blackest ones:
All the unstated bargains, but I would not

Plead. The effect was coriolus—the whirlpool
Of them turning backwards, that pause,

Silence, vibrato, a whole concert of evasive
Violins and calculations. The ghost frowned

And said, *I told you so.* Yes, and each time I start
From a dream, I need gauze to bandage wounds.

That young woman with full breasts, two firm
Nipples to suck. Well . . . how could he resist?

Knit & Purl

At six (when they told me I was too young)
I taught myself to knit using two pencils

And a ball of string. With the glaze and gaze
Of time, I see it was essential to make

Something from nothing—to weave a basket
Of seaweed, test lightning, bake challah,

Unwind a cocoon, challenge the status quo.
Never to drift and purl downstream with ease.

Purl & UnKnit

Whatever is most difficult must be tried. Purl
Instead of knit. Find the prize in Cracker Jack

Without tearing the box. Do *tour jetés en pointe*
Until mustered out. Swim until done in.

If creatures lurk beneath the hawthorne, catch
Them, pinch out their dark secrets. And when

It's time to put pen to paper—when I put pen to
Paper—I must be ruthless: unknit and imperil.

Warp & Woof

The ghost of yesterday is in the garden
Cleaning his nails with a silver file. He says

The camelias and hosta are lush this year,
But the red squirrels need to be shot.

I'm on ice skates trying to race away from him,
On stilts anxious to rise to another plane, but he's

Picked up a bagpipe and is warping and woofing
Until its clamor makes it impossible to think.

Who is that man, he barks, between the wheeze of
Pipes, and what do you think you are doing?

Woof & Warp

In the background, a chorus hallelujahs in some
Language I don't speak—Greek perhaps—

As the texture on the loom exchanges thick for
Thin. A thread breaks. Then another. Now

What? I ask the ghost, but instead of replying
With words, he uses his hands to sign. He may be

Saying dog or god, love or lust. Looming above,
He pokes my chest with his silver nail file.

He may be saying the game is not worth the candle
Or just telling me to file this one away.

Appled & Snaked

Please leave before I ask you again
To conjure moon mares with me, before

You juggle one more vow. Once I mistook
Fantasy for reality. Then a mythic garden

Grew around us as we slept—appled and
Snaked until I felt rooted there,

Until, though unclothed and unhoused, I
Was reluctant to lift my feet and flee.

Snaked & Appled

Please leave before I begin again to cry
Over our spilled honey, before

The bees swarm, before I start to
Count chickens as well as snakes and

Apples, before my thoughts are naked
As my scarred body. Because, if you

Don't, I may break my silence, break you, too,
As I strike through this overgrown dream.

Live & Learn

The ghost of yesterday is lobbing blue hailstones
In my direction. Cease & desist, he tells me,

Sounding like my dead father. Fish or cut bait,
Eat or be eaten. Now the ghost

Flashes past on my father's speed skates. Then he's
In a ballroom waltzing with Aunt Dorothy.

Once, allowed, I'd slip 20s from Father's wallet,
Pretend I didn't see when he and Mother jerked

Apart as I entered their room. No fireflies, so what
Do I have? His pinwheel, his silver nail file?

Learn & Live

Rise & shine, the ghost/father says. Early bird gets.
Stand & deliver. Divide & conquer. Hear the piano?

The question is: how did the ghost revive the lily,
And am I the lily? Surely not a shrinking violet.

I learned that one. Nor do I walk or throw like a girl.
Fire & ice cause trouble, I know, and don't put

Too many eggs in a basket. But he—impatient ghost—
Leaves before I can find out about pain & loss,

About how to capture a firefly that isn't there,
How to keep its small pulse of luminescence.

Curved Space

Living in Curved Space

She inhales stars until she is light-filled
and can bat-wing above the dark earth.

Another out-of-body sequence and
her flanks fur, throat chuffs, tail grows.

As a fish shifts color when it fins from light
into shadow or a chameleon on a twig she

stretches herself on a Persian carpet until
she absorbs its bright and dusky tones,

its curlicues, swags, and feathered wreaths
and is invisible to those who come for her.

Below the high dam, the real Abu-Simbel lies.
Below the sea, the lighthouse of Pharos.

There are worlds, too—under lava, under ice—
where no tree falls and no sound is heard.

What is hidden will not again be visible. She
seeks refuge in these places: angles of repose

where salmon turn to seagulls and a hand
may, to infinity, hold a pen and draw itself.

First Memory

There was a dripping spigot and another girl,
her name the same as mine.
Her Dutched hair, size, and smocked dress
mimicked me.
But I held no Dy-Dee doll with
cherub mouth, whose red-nippled bottle
tasted like gum, smelled like tricycle tires;
so with stealth I stalked that doppelgänger.
Patient even then, waiting until our mothers,
voices braided into impenetrable strands,
receded I struck.
Swift and vicious, I prized the bottle from that girl,
shattered it on the pavement.
As she wailed, I—anxious to possess
beauty—scooped up fistfuls of new-made diamonds,
unconcerned by needles of pain
or bright leakage between my fingers.

The Man Who Stood on a Chair

In 1929, my father hung up his skates,
red-pencilled one last *Daily Cardinal,*
leased himself to the family business.
Given the year, writing the great American
novel was not an option. So making way for
Bellow and Malamud, my father rented flats,
sublet the Olive Street store to Sol Jacobs
who sold suits with two pairs of trousers.

By the time I began to take notice
he was a job-curdled man
who escaped each night to the arms of
a La-Z-Boy where, as images blurred on TV,
he thumbed through *Life.* Inflated from
skating-trim to a mid-life 190, lamenting
wheel shimmy in his Olds 88 or a bogie
on the dog-leg 17th, he exuded a Babbit-y aura.

Then last fall in Santa Monica, 13 years after
his death, I crashed a party
and met a man from Missouri who told me
of the night my father stood on a chair.
At a banquet where each person was asked
to say his name, someone's grandson
had stood on a chair to introduce himself.
Then my father, chuckling, had done the same.

That night in my hotel, unable to find sleep
or the phantom who had been my father,
I chased down dark corridors, searching.
Toward morning, maddened by half-cracked doors,
I knew I'd never catch the man—
novelist *manqué,* streak of the Silver Skates,
who wrote STET on galleys or had the spontaneity
to confront 300 people standing on a chair.

Minimalism

Chicago, my mother, sister, and I
were taking one last trip:
the Art Institute to see my cousin's show.
Tom, a mimimalist—only 30 and
already a star—sculpts with string,
pencil-shavings, aspirin, bubble gum,
mucus, soap, pubic hair.

Tulips, daffodils, and pear trees were
blooming outside, and inside
hotel walls were rampant with roses.
At night, my sister and I sprawled on
flowered beds like young girls as
Mother sat on a loveseat in a purple gown
flaking skin from her legs. They
were swollen, studded with keloids,
and I stared at them as her voice
gravelled on reliving dinner, the art show,
other dinners and shows and clothing,

other wallpapers remembered from
long-vanished rooms. She sat talking
until the carpet at her feet
was white with a thousand petals
of dead skin. *Look,* she said, as she
rose to pick her way to her room,
I've snowed all over your floor . . . .

When morning came and I paused
by the loveseat to tie my shoes,
my sister cringed and told me
I was standing on
Mother's body. As I side-stepped
toward the window, gazed out
at pear blossoms clouding a fierce
spring wind, my sister covered
our mother with Sunday funnies
and said we'd better not call Tom.

Boundary Waters

I was guiding a trip where a young boy drowned.
Near Ely, he knifed into yellow-green,
stroked past humped boulders and never came up.

Then a second boy donned goggles and angled
himself deep where schools of dark fish finned.
I watched, held my breath, waited,

saying, *This is taking too long.* Goggles bobbed up,
but not his head, and he was lost to me, also.
I told myself, *This is not true, only a dream,*

and so I undrowned him, summoned him back to
balance on gunwales, a delicate, sinewy form,
skin stretched taut over ribcage. As I watched, he

dove and swam, rising again and again from
a bottomless lake. Then I summoned the first boy
until, water dribbling from hair and shoulders,

he stood before me, gave me a zippered pouch.
In it, crimped bills and fragments of cold
rock crystal. Turning away from boundary waters,

I mounted a horse, pulled one boy to the saddle
behind me, then the other. Wind and grit
in teeth, I loped through forests of jack pine

feeling water sucked from my clothing. The boys
dried, too, growing lighter until they, like birchbark,
peeled and peeled and flaked away to nothing.

Winter Solstice

1. Baba

In the cellar, on a rusted lawn chair
beside the water heater, I find
our Baba. Wearing black lace-ups
with cubed heels, a dress with
handsewn buttonholes — identical except
where her waist makes one grin,
she stares at me until hectic spots stain
cheeks. Light penetrates high,
fly-specked windows and illuminates
hairnet spider-webbing
her forehead below folds of
pale sheitel. Around her: detritus
of decades. Our cellar is for things
which have no use. First we stockpile
them at the stairs. Then by the door.
At last, below, they molder on shelves
or on the child-sized workbench:
a drum, old Lincoln Logs, last year's
cancelled checks. Eyes passing over
all, aware of heat and drip of
water heater, I stare again at Baba.
What are you doing in the cellar? I ask.
Rolling socks, she tells me. *Like most*
bubbes I stay at home and roll socks.
Now her cheeks deepen. *Or sometimes,*
at night, I roll in sweet-scented hay . . . .

Baba, it's dark and damp,
I tell her. *You don't belong down here.*
She smiles, layers one thick-fingered hand
over the other. *But I do, my Dumpling,*
she replies slowly, *because upstairs*
in your fine house, I forget to
roll and can't ever remember my name.

2. Mother

Poised before her scale, Mother — arbiter
of family myths — weighs truth against
fabrication. *But it never happened,*
she insists, balancing her perceptions,
discarding mine. *Baba*
was Grampa Jack's mother's mother,
dead before you were born.

                    Still, I insist, *she was*
there, sitting in the dark dressed in
worsted. With hands shaped like mine,
and a long face. She spoke to me.

Mother, unwilling to pardon unreality,
adjusts her blindfold, recalibrates,
scoffs at me. *Then it's*
her photograph you remember.
Just a picture. We used to store it in
the cellar wedged between
our old furnace and the hot water heater.

3. Self

Shuffle, step, shuffle, step. Down in
the cellar I am tapping out all the bright
things Mother and everyone tell me
are not true. *Shuffle, scuff, turn.*
Look at me. Then look again.
My cane, my hat—both are props,
for I am not yet Baba, not yet my mother.
Still, upstairs, I can't practice on
satin-finish floors, because I'll scar them.
So, between furnace and water heater,
using the workbench as barre,
I dance.

I dance against time, against rage. Days
are short now.

        Baba danced in Szumsk,
I'm sure, but never here. Looking on,
she finds me as disconcerting as my house:
strong-hipped, grown woman in black
skivvies, socks, and TeleTones tapping
into gathering darkness. *Why?* she asks.
Because, I answer, eyeing squared hands.
Shuffle, flap. Shuffle-hop, toe.
Because as winter comes, I, too, need
time—*shuffle, roll*—to contemplate
sweet-scented hay.

Forgiveness

Sometimes, I buy old quilts but never ones
with any stain. No tea, no blood,
or fluids that will not yield to Tide.
This quilt, held by a woman from
Missouri, is Ocean Waves, 1890—white
with hand-dipped blue,

a triangulated flow of motion. Yet when we
(the woman from Missouri and I)
sail the quilt on her clothesline, there,
on the crest of a wave, is a mark.
India ink. Indelible.

The ink, I'm sure (men do not write in bed),
was dropped by a woman. I stare until
I see someone who dreamed oceans
and words. Pillow-propped, her fingers
calloused from milking and stitch-pitted,
she scrawled, stole time to

piece thoughts. But the quilt has a stain.
No, I say. Then that quilter
squints across time, summons me.
As she beckons
with her pen, a single drop falls.

Stained, I murmur, undulated by
Ocean Waves. The woman
from Missouri is speaking,
but her words lap past me as I hear only
the other one, the one with the pen.
Head, hand, heart, she urges. *Courage.*

I nod. Then, for what we cannot
change, I forgive us both.

Camera Obscura

She waits in darkness staring down
at the parabola of wave, sand, gull, and rock.
Views shift clockwise and clockwise, breakers siphon
off the curved lip, until the world is upsidedown
yet circling endlessly to re-right itself.
A pelican skids, beaks a fish, wings over the rim
of the silken bowl. A thin woman dressed
in black, who might be herself, descends stairs
and vanishes in the Musée Mechanique.

Leonardo knew this camera. Vermeer used it
for portraits: a spinning mirror
and lenses—one convex, one concave.
As light glints through an aperture,
a picture roils upon a curve in a dim room.
Standing there watching her spouse and children
rotate out of sight on the beach below,
she feels herself begin to invert
and slide off the surface into nothingness

or coexistence. Leaving the camera, she climbs
to the street and a car hits her. Standing at the curb,
she sees a car hit someone else.
She steps in front of a car and no impact jars.
But maybe she never moved at all. Music, odd and
cymbal-like, dins her head. Moments peel off: history
of what happens or what might be. Perhaps she
can choose memory. Elect the outcome,
dismiss the accident, moment of rape or desertion?

Her children, robust and long-limbed, cavort
yet orbit ever further off the smooth edges
of the arc. Each rotation they are changed,
color-leached, flatter, more distant.
Her husband riffles pages of his paper yet stares
outward toward the breaker line where a windsurfer
luffs a waxy sail. This man with newspaper
is a white-haired stranger in polarfleece.
She might abandon the dark room and meet him

on the beach. She might, like the woman in black,
glide into the Musée, face Laughing Sal's
day-glo ringlets and lewd-jiggle cantaloupe breasts.
Or she may risk the path of the oncoming car,
cross the street and dissolve,
leaving everything and everyone
capsized in the oceanic curve of time.

Undercut

We're holding hands, breathing hard.
The overhang, a limestone cliff,
part of a mountain, should last forever,
yet as we pause here—rock can't
withstand the persistence of water—
the creek is claiming it.

Basins are rounded by it, polished
until we shield our eyes in sunlight.
The glacial-tinted falls
slowly scours a wider hole.
Above us, fever of red-orange lichen
and firs awed by silvered moss.

Below, the canyon's deepest cut,
once limestone, now only space.
Each year the creek-song grows fainter.
While we stand gazing down, rock is
disappearing. Nothing is static.
Not lichen, not fir, not water, not breath.

Women Lit/Unlit

Tess

— Vale of Blackmoor

Any country girl should
grasp the difference between hay and straw,
between provisions and residue. "Waste not,
want not," my simple mother often said.
"And remember the golden rule . . . ."
Yet she failed to speak of alchemy or fate.

One Mayday as straw flecked beneath my feet,
I, beribboned, danced
following an elusive skein,
a reeling cat's-eye taw,
until, slippers shredded, I heard bells chiming
while roosters gloated past the sunrise.
Then hidden by a bough,
languishing on hay, I endeavored to spin
gold. I persisted until,
disheartened,
I tendered chicory to the hens.

Soon the ailing hens refused to lay,
and my father whispered, "Damaged goods."
Later, he sighed, "Straw. Straw . . . ."

Ophelia

— *Elsinore*

She woke to a mocking bird and sensed a lucky day.
Face decaled against panes, she browsed
the morning. Unjacketed, she flung herself past
blue door and gate, skinked across the grass
to where he lay, coiled, waiting.
Unsifted, she offered rosemary, pansies. Unsifted,
she exulted when hair tangled to silken knots and
stockings pleated at her ankles. *I love you,* she
breathed, then breathed it again, thirsty for
his reply. But as he rolled her
in grass cuttings, she felt tiny sharpened spears
prick, draining away green, fading all to brown.

Hester's Grammar

—Boston

I lay my skirt across a chair and it lies there. (Present)
I laid my slippers on the floor and they lay there. (Past)
I have laid myself upon a quilt and I have lain there. (Perfect)

He lays his pants by my skirt and they lie there. (Present)
He laid his boots beside my slippers and they lay there. (Past)
He has laid his body next to mine and it has lain there. (Perfect)

Lay, lies,
laid, lay
laid, lain.
All grammatically correct and, still, it is not
the lay or laid that bothers him but the lies.

He may love to lie with me, yet to lie about me is for him
a tense not found in any text of standard usage. (Imperfect)

Bertha Mason's Sonnet

—Thornfield Hall

Flames seep yellowed blood across the heath.
Back-lit, a water-marked silhouette floats,
is consumed. Eerie to feel nostrils pinched
by reek, yet be too numbed to know
its menace. A cricket, cymballing legs, sings
in the glade. For sanctuary, I, too, sing.
As fire plumes, it purifies, creating
refuge where sheep may safely graze.
Anxious to drown madding cries,
I lullaby the night, ask absolution.
Muffled sanity is all I seek. But lured by
embers, swallowed then
released, I phoenix from the ashes
aware rapture, like pain, is seldom earned.

Anna

— Moscow

Above our bed, an invisible mesh
of hairnet seines brittle-gray curls.
A head without a body bobs
as hands with no arms ripple air.

That face looms, and insomnia sucks
like a slick freshwater eel. Afraid,
I cry, "Who are you? What do you want?"
Then with my nails, I rake at flesh

until eyes float the night—eyes hazed
by a film of years; and, at last, I know
that woman.
She sees why I can't dream. Gazing

at me angled by your body, she feels
my restlessness, my pain; and, neither
curious nor gloating, she says,
"I remember loving. I remember love."

Emma

— Yonville L'Abbaye

The place we use has public stairs
where red-swirled carpet flaunts
lost knots of hair while coughing up
the smell of Tuesday's cabbage.

In my dreams, when we lie together,
our place is green and slick as pond ice;
and Mother forgetful of my husband,
appears greeting us benignly.

Other guests wander by. Mother serves
canapes. Guests eat. They drink.
Their smiles illuminate dark corners.
And as we touch, they observe.

But soon the frozen algae softens
from our warmth, thawing the dream place
until it begins to threaten
wisps of hair, whiffs of cabbage.

Lena

—Yoknapatawpha County

"Pickup, pick up them broken pieces
and take them to the Lord . . . . "

Shadowdappled womanflesh—
something moving forever and without
progress across an urn.

Under a jonquilcolored sun,
in too-big man's shoes, she walks,
placid, face smooth
as a stone yet not hard. Appreciative
because people can be kind,

she chooses to be surprised by passion,
fecundity, sweetsuckling
of a brier-patch child.
She may be *a forgotten bead*
from a broken string; but dreaming

moongleamed shapes, she—aware
of train whistles at a crossing miles away—
carries on.

"Pickup, pick up them broken pieces
and take them to the Lord . . . . "

Molly Has the Last Word

—7 Eccles Street, Dublin

Yes love lovers frigging sex the smell of a man
thats all anyone ever supposes I think about
dresses perfume flesh roses men getting up under
my petticoats and giving kisses
long and hot down to my soul and forget that like
other women I am sensitive can cry
yet you see I know more than most because of the word
because I read and have not only a soul but
grey matter too like the men
o rocks I may not know metempsychosis still with Calypso
barelolling above my brass bed I know winedark seas
have my own copy of Lord Byrons poems
as well as three pairs of gloves
lying here Ive read Wilkie Collins Moonstone
Rabelais East Lynne almost any book as long as it
hasnt a Molly in it
and bytheby have a passing acquaintance with Jane
Emma Tess Anna and some of their sisters
even if theyre all afraid to say what I say except
maybe Dame Alys of Bath for she like me is
yes earthy honest and somewhat taken with a bit of lace
a nice sort of brooch or young loins
and would know how to act when a man wanted to
milk her sweet and thick into his tea
but come from another time she hasnt had to listen to

bumgut filthyminded Dr Freud seen him kick up
a row trying to find out what it is women want
though he never asked me
yes of course I could have told him yes
for with my life and reading and knowing
women are sisters under their skins
this answers simple like the nose on his face and it is
power yes power we want
then people would be a fat lot better
and youd never again see this much killing or drunkeness
so power it is in love in sex in war and you can
go all the way back if you wish to the ancient Greeks
to those sisters Fates Muses Seaside girls and the rest
yes for they knew what they wanted as I know what I want
power but particularly the power
men have been least willing to give us
still with a red Andalusian rose in my hair I will possess it yes
the power of the word
yes thats what women want yes the word yes

Fire Is Favorable to the Dreamer

Love of Lost Time

Notice the tree of discarded leaves
bent by the river where a woman holds a line.

Metaphors hardly visible,
shadings of weight, pauses in tone,
flick of memory,
as the river yields light and motion
of current.

She never tried to triumph in whitewater
or upon sheer faces of rock.
Instead, fading pictures
where slouch and grace showed them
all without clothes,

sharing ripe fruit,
as, one by one, they traded images,
dropped numbered expectations
while cast off pips
bobbed drunkenly downstream.

Love of lost time is a bottomless eddy
where her line will circle and keep on circling.

Baggage

I pack my trunk, and in it I put—
my China doll, my trading cards, my ice skates . . . .

a child's game, once played in many languages and now
for real. Since love draws goods and chattel,
today my trunk is heavy. Then black dogs summon
white nights while I long for weightless flight.

Sleepless, I make lists—like Cousin Bertha who has
the longest Life List of any living Midwestern woman.
But my numbered flocks do not fly free.
Days they scritch for seed about my feet.
At night, still active, they chirrup in the Douglas fir,
and as hearts flail against hollow bones
they peel away threads of my flesh.

Oriana Fallaci says she can sit weeks, months, smoking,
drinking coffee, writing as the Berlin Wall falls
and uprisings bloody Tiananmen Square. Oriana has
no trunk, no homing flock with a taste for suet.

But I pack my trunk and in it I put—
their old skates and mittens, their lists and mine.

Eye of the Water Lily

Night is approaching. The air scented
and pollened yellow.
Edges are indistinct.
Surrounded by an O'Keefe blossom
with fierce stamens, dappled, gnat-freckled,
she's furled by the lily.
There, folded into the rods and cones
of its golden eye,
a spiral of light cushions the air.
No longer restless, she draws up
her knees, idles where
beauty is pure and joy has form.

This is where she was before she began,
in darkness, knees to her chest,
a rounded, rose-nippled girl-seed
not yet desperate for light.
Dreaming of liquid warmth
and gentle hands, knowing only the imprint
of calyx and pistil,
of unrealized petals.
Damp and smooth and unsuspecting.
Not yet impatient
for ripeness, not yet rooting
wildly toward an idea of flower.

From the Wing Bone of a Crane

Anemophiles, lovers of wind, believe time
is infinite, and the past has no claim,

but in China there's a 9,000 year old flute
carved from the wing bone of a crane.

Once, at Jiahu in the Yellow River Valley,
flood and ebb, rice ribboned green, and crane

on one leg in the shallows, his target-red eye
scanning fish. A rock flies. Feathered death.

O solemn bone, white and hollow and smooth.
Seven chiseled holes, a delicate windy sound,

millennium after millennium lost
only to be unearthed, brown and mottled,

trilled again by other lips and fingers.
Same flute. Different song.

The human brain weighs little and is lightly
grooved, yet it knows when a flute is a flute.

Anemophiles might embrace this bone.
Or say it does not, cannot possibly exist.

River of Milky Light

Furled in a blue dream, trimmed and wicked,
Ophelia beams through a pathless graveyard

where leaf and branch tremble with mad light
as sky-swatches drift slowly down.

Stretching up, afraid to breathe, she juggles
beauty on the tips of her fingers.

Don't go away, she whispers. *Suspense is all.*
Tonight, everything lost must be returned.

But while archer and huntress prowl
with a river of blue-starred light between them,

she stumbles, drops rosemary, violets, rue,
and thyme black as her shadow.

When she bends forward to seine them—
nonny, hey nonny—from the river, she catches

herself reflected there. Reaching out and down,
she and her mirror-image embrace:

blue-black lovers, their dreams unfurled,
wet and weightless in currents of milky light.

Kursk Good-Bye

Nadia, my cabbage, don't think of me here in the underworld
without you. Think of the Chagall print over our bed
with its bride and groom and wild-eyed blue cow.

Yes, love, your worst nightmares have become real.
Our submarine at the bottom of the Barents Sea.
Explosions, fire, flooding—only a handful still alive.
Emergency lights are dimming. Soon they'll fail.
We're short on oxygen, leaking.
Here in the ninth compartment, many are injured,
others weeping and clutching one another.
Vlady has soiled himself. Dmitri is writing a poem.
We've no way to surface, so there will be no escape.

And me? I'm here yet not here, listening for chords of
that symphony you like—Rachmaninoff, maybe,
where bells ring out at the end. Music might make me
forget your grandmother's featherbeds,
berries we'll never pick, latchkeys we will not lose,
children who won't know "Eyewinker" and "Chinchopper."
Oh, Nadia, we never got to Petersburg or Istanbul.
We never tasted artichoke or caviar,
never caught fireflies or rode a toboggan,
but enchanted by Chagall, we laughed,
and, freed from laws of gravity and common sense,
we held hands, rose up and saw our town, its pathways,
its chicks and chickens, as we floated above rooftops.
Together we were weightless, loving ourselves
and each other inside our paperweight world.

A world too young to turn real. Too new for you to carp
about mildewed clothes, how I chewed food,
how you felt when I took you from behind. No ridicule
for the uselessness of the skinny egret I whittled
from the handle of a mop; but Nadia, the lights are
hissing. It's, at the same time, hot and cold. More water.
Now the lights *are* out. Ivan has a torch, but I
am writing blindly, touching myself with my left hand,
thinking of you. Pretend I am not under water
but on a black raft, afloat on an endless tropical sea
with black breakers and black palms waving overhead,
and you're here. It's your hand, your mouth
I feel in this obscene darkness. Yes—but wait—
look — the black sky is lightening, and I hear bells,
all the bells of Russia are ringing
and ringing out at once, and we are not, after all,
on a raft but on the back of a wild-eyed blue cow,
cantering across the arc of night sky

as dandelions of light burst before our eyes,
and the bells, they are vibrating, shaking, shaking
us both, and, Nadia, Nadia—do you hear them? Do you—

Mary Todd Lincoln at Ford's Theatre

So I said no, no more dramas like these with pieces of my flesh
being peeled away by birds of prey, and, still, I put on
the black-and-white striped silk and, on my head, black lace,
but other than that
it was a night like many with the walls closing in on me
and sound of rat tails in the walls and spiders and roaches
streaming over inked velvet, and so I said *Stop* and *Let it stop now,*
because I have exhausted my strength for others' freedom—
you see, I was a Southern girl raised right, though morbidly,
and did what my father said, was gracious to the dark-skinned,
met their eyes and gave them their due,
for a good Christian soul should not shirk but give all
good measure, and so I gave and give to them now, give to
the President who owns my life and my sons
(though the Lord took two back) and to the world, too,
letting everyone enter to pick at strips of tender skin,
but other than that what
has it gotten me but here and here and here, play within a play,
into this dark box where I sit holding the President's hand,
corseted, constricted by time and chance, my hair tight-pinned
under its grieving-Madonna drape while my head swells
and I feel stings as hordes of bees begin to siphon honey
from my eyes and ears, from my breasts and beneath my skirts,
and though I should be grateful and say blessed be the sinners,
blessed be those who hear the call of duty,
blessed be the free hearts of those with skin black as coal,
but other than that
if there were a way to stop my life I would—no, I do not lie,
and I would, if I had my father's Derringer and a bullet here,
put a stop to the shrinking walls and birds of prey,

to rats and roaches, spiders and bees, to the vanishing skin,
and I'd draw a Kentucky bead and *Bang* I'd say,
because as every Christian is capable of love, so is he capable
of murder as am I, and I'd put an end to this suffering
but other than that
why shouldn't it be now before I am stripped to sinew and bone,
before it is only my bones that can dance, only bones of fingers
left to grasp the President's own, and then there will be
no more endurance at this interminable play and my role will
be unlearned and undone because what I say will not be
long-remembered, and it can, if I act, stop
in an hour, in a scene, in a minute, in a heartbeat . . .
but other than that
now that they, the other dark ones, have been freed, let me, too,
be freed from myself and from this killing darkness—*Bang*.

Death of a Podiatrist

Please don't laugh. This is serious.
I was at a play and Arthur Miller, too,
though it wasn't his. On stage,
there was a cast, solemn and intent,
lines learned, places blocked out,
a grave business, and I thought
it was *House of Mirth*, and that was
Lily Bart up there kicking back her train
with one foot and skirting danger.
Surrounding her were men—
middle-aged and graying—their lives:
old coins, minted, dated, clinking ominously
as they moved together and apart,
but then I was with them
on stage, and Lily Bart was nowhere
to be seen though I had her purse.
The metallic sound swelled until
I could feel weight, taste copper
on my tongue. Still, it wasn't me
in danger but a man who looked like
Willy Loman in a morning coat
growing thinner and less commanding,
dying before my eyes.
I knew and loved him, yet all I did was
change costume from white to red,
put the purse on the chair at stage right,
walk through a practiced pattern
that pretended to be real life.
Lights shifted. Though I was spotlighted,
the man was not. Checks and balances
changed. Doorways darkened, and my feet,
in Lily's high-heeled slippers, hurt.
I needed help, but the lines weren't mine.
This was the death of a podiatrist.
A podiatrist? I don't know why.
But please don't laugh. This is serious.

Marilyn M. Thinks About French & Russian Dogs

Du Chien
a French phrase (that can't really be translated)—
used to describe Tolstoy's wife
and sometimes me, since I want
to be a Tolstoy heroine—
is supposed to be about sexiness:
avoir d'élégance, de la séduction.
But I think, after all,
it's only another way of pointing out
who a man might tame
or teach to fetch
one who can learn on command
come, sit, stay, lie down, shake hands
someone to pet but one happy
with bones tossed in her direction
and she'll follow his lead
play dumb, play dead
entertain him
walk by his side, get the paper
accept scraps, beg for treats, for affection
lick him with her rough pink tongue
invite him to enter from behind
warm his bed, stay home
waiting for him to reappear
obey, fetch, speak when prompted
know her place
be grateful yet like a wolf
be dangerous
capable of sinking fangs into his throat.
Du chien has possibilities, I think,
but it does when used by a man
still mean *doggy* and, also, *bitch* . . . .

The Last Time This Water Saw Land,
It Was in Africa

The last time this parrot saw fish,
it was flying over an island purpled by sunset.
The last time this pebble skipped across
a white sand beach, it was tossed
by a man with a parrot on his shoulder
and a fish in his creel.
The last time this key saw a lock,
I was on an island with the man, the parrot, the creel,
the fish, and a hot golden ball at the horizon.
But winds were fierce, the man and the light
unforgiving. So I shook
sand from my shoes, locked my suitcase,
and caught a plane.
In my hand, one smooth pebble
and a notebook lined with Caribbean clichés.

Janis Says: *Burn, Baby, Burn*

Stars splash from the wake of a steep blue sky
And stripes furrow flesh scored with blood
Stars orbit the full moons of my ass
And stripes jack the twin suns of my tits
Stars trail barbs of light through fields of weed
Stripes bleed like acid-pricked skin
Stars forfeit their edges one by one
Stripes flay themselves into raveling nooses
Stars round and wide-eyed now boom the music of the spheres.

In the rockets' red glare I pledge allegiance to the flag
And to myself and long may we wave
My country wrong or wrong   God damn America
He's not *my* Uncle Sam
The rain which should be cold is scalding me
In amber waves flame sucks flame

As flames spark from eyes and mouth
They splash orbit trail forfeit boom
They furrow jack bleed flay scorch
Melting stars melding stripes fusing sky and earth and flesh
Because I'm hot so combustibly hot

Burn and let the swords melt to ploughshares
And let stripes sweep from sea to fucking sea
And let stars smoke upwards into twisted galaxies

Is anybody listening

We have bared our souls and our bodies
So we can dip ourselves in this fresh fire
So we can sing God Bless America
Sing O say can you see *and rest here when day is done*

1981: Sprite Lost, Sprite Found

Liberty. In God we trust. Or distrust.
This penny is dangerous. Minted the year my daughter was lost.
Beware of tube tops, lug-soled boots. Beware of ear piercing:
the more holes, the more trouble leaks out.
Trouble was the blue hair. The pink. The aubergine.
Fashion pages. Mirrors. Bikinis. Dope.
The boy with dreadlocks. The river guide. Magic mushrooms.

Lincoln's looking on in profile. His lips thin as is he.
As thin as she was. Honest Abe thought I could not tell a lie,
but I did, for when she began to starve herself,
I lost all liberty, all God-trust. There was no God.
In 1981, nothing was real but her skeletal hands
and coppery metallic breath upon my neck. Each night, in secret,
I poured out liters of saccharined diet drink
and refilled them with sugared Sprite to bring her—
my hardest, brightest, thinnest penny—back alive.

Getting Tattooed the Hard Way

After the surgery where they took the breast tissue
and the nipple, after they twisted a back muscle
across my chest, grafted skin for an areola,
they cut a fishtail, used
a purse-string stitch to form a small bud.

This they tattooed into a lovely pink rose.
Pigment and palette: Beige 10, Beige 1, Pink 1, Brown 2.
A numb rose, artificial on a man-made hill.
A Rubenesque body, injured Mona Lisa smile.

The landscape is a dream, benign fields of
tufted cotton where I'm searching
for someone who's lost, a white labyrinth
with a mirror; and when I turn a corner, I'm walking
unclothed into an counterfeit image.

Scar tissue is stronger than flesh yet weaker, too.
Hedge-clipper hum of needle. Sting of punctured flesh.
There's the rosebud, but how can I tender it?
A Rubenesque body, angry Mona Lisa smile.

Trespass Into Morning

Don't awaken me. I'm walking out of my night
into the dark matter of your dreams.
Pinwheels of fluorescence disguise me
as I trespass. You: hot and trusting

on your back, like a careless cat, breath faint,
your unmarked face exposing
the lie of decadence. *And so, love,*
why am I here, and what am I meant to do?

Olive-skinned girl and boy with blonde curls
are eyeing us. Your children? Mine?
Or ourselves thrust forward
in clothes exhausted from another life?

Hand in hand the two poise in the doorway,
watching me watching you, as pinwheels coalesce
into wings, and fireflies
rise up to stun the air between us.

Avalanche Warning

Sleep is shifting away. Under the dark cave
of blankets, a man's body by mine.
But it is snowing here. Yes, in our room, cold flakes
sluice from the high white ceiling.
Unseen crystals crown my head, dissolve
and run down my cheek. Though motionless,
I am aware of the snow as it continues
to fall.

                       Tasting snow on my tongue,
smelling its metallic freshness, I rise. Behind me
in bed, the safe silhouette of the sleeping man;
but I am in danger. Drifts scud at the windows
and door as I remember the Siq at Petra,
the eclipse on the Altiplano.
If I stay here, I'll become an ice maiden,
a weightless shadow of white, and there's
some place else I need to be. By the bed where
the man's rough breath

                       trolls through cold-flaked air,
I strap on crampons, shrug into my pack.
Wait for me, I whisper, reaching to twist fingers
in his steel-wool hair. *But forgive me.*
For I am not yet done. Then peering through goggles
to ward off blindness, I step past swales of
blue-white snow and alone in the dark begin to climb.

Fire Is Favorable

To Dream Your Slippers Are Much Admired
Foretells You Will Be Involved in a Flirtation
That Will Bring Disgrace

They weren't soft squirrel fur or glass like Cinderella's,
but passionfruit red, and they waltzed her past
mirrors while everyone watched her feet.
Desperate to escape interiors for a life of the flesh,
she found herself butterflied in a meadow
as someone else's love poured wine and fed her berries.
Then exotic sites with strange customs. White peaks
and dark wells. Desert dunes, sea-stacks, a gypsy campfire.
Hammocks, lean-tos. Someone else's love now hers.
Moonlight leaking between trees and starlight from
the edge of time

                until her slippers were worn at the heel,
sole-thinned, warped by rain and mud.
As foolish onlookers eyed them, her mother wailed:
"You play with fire. Now you're damaged goods
and can't ever come home."

To Dream of Black Swans Denotes Illicit Pleasures

They were swimming in the lagoon, sculling
as they eased under the arched bridge reflected
among clouds on the still surface of morning.
Not a presence, more of an absence, empty space
where the sun was a ball of cold glass. Dark feathers
in the air, necks arched, mouths open, aching for
any tomorrow. A time of no time, mirrored eyes
reflecting only the present. Together, a sense of
burning—now, yet never again. Then water roiled,
lily pads entangled their feet, and a voice said,

"Stop this . . . ." So she changed the dream, denied it,
ignored stone and leaf and glass,
reversed the negative, insisting and insisting
those sleek, insubstantial swans were always white.

Fire Is Favorable to the Dreamer
If She doesn't Get Burned

Cradle-rocker, quilt-maker, bread-baker, wife.
When she gave up wanderlust and the hour of the wolf,
settled for a white bed and fire in the hearth,
she sat before it unable to read the future in its flames.
Many chicks but one rooster, a shankbone in the pot.
Bottle-scrubber, boot-blacker, fresh-diaper, snot-wiper.
Floor-mopper, leaf-raker, candlestick-maker.
Gardener, scarecrow, drudge. Berry-minder, button-finder.
Body-double, dreamer. Sleep-walker, schemer.
Angel and whore. Keeper of the flame.
Still, the bread wouldn't brown, jam wouldn't jell,
and, when the six-toed cat birthed a two-headed kitten,
lightning struck, leaving more fires to quench.
But as she beat at flames, her face was roughed
by fine grit, etching the spirit and the skin.

To Dream of Eating Vegetables
Is an Omen of Strange Luck

First the leeks and eggplant, then the broccoli and a need
to consume it. Brussels sprouts leeching water
an acrid brown or summer squash pulped into paste,
and she was forking them up, greedy and heedless.

As she knelt among carrots, eager to taste tops
and all, she considered *the stone, the leaf,*
the unfound door, examined a moth-shaped bruise
waiting for it to fly away. And when she looked up,
he was there—almost-forgotten—seasoned now,
heading toward her, his face stenciled
with morning light, arms heavy with strings
of peppers. "Why have you come? she asked.

"To open the door," he said, festooning her with peppers.
Then, when he stroked her bruise with the tip of
his thumb, they crossed a threshhold,
stepped past leaf and stone, and began to dance.

Archeology of Falling

there's nothing to prove she begins
this is not a competition you have to win

in the ancient cistern in Istanbul

it's an exploration she continues
a landscape of foreign complexities
of the unexamined

Medusa her proud head and neck — a column

all I ask is two things she whispers
as over and over the possibilities replay themselves

snake hair wide eyes green with time

no lies and unconditional love
he's listening yet laughing pursuing archeology
the unexamined vessel the hidden smile

stone-face turned herself to stone

a delicate probe she murmurs chance
and the deceit of darkness and light

underwater submerged upside-down smiling

and afterwards she says there is
no afterwards new territory old loss
leave the stone unturned

visible yes but still forever a loss

Fallen Light

The mile-long breakers threaded north-south
thump against the western shore.

An afternoon of little wind and the shook foil
of water is sparked by a thousand fallen suns.

In their brilliance, I try to measure December's
failing days, anxious to hold them and seine

agates, shells, ancient sand dollar fossils
roiling invisibly below the surf.

Never assume, I remind myself kneeling on iceplant,
because all beauty is promised to darkness

as quartz and granite are ground to sand,
so a life erodes beneath breakers and fallen light;

yet, when the sun is low, even a single grain of sand
casts an angular, heart-stopping shadow.

Natural Defenses

What Has Been Lost:

Star-wishes, the courage to step on a crack.

How to speak with innocence,
wait at someone's feet, follow deer through brush.
To apologize and mean it.

Baby teeth in the silk pouch,
the scientist who wrote his own obituary,
Father and his father, the delicate touch of a fingertip,
the diamond pin, the right breast.

Map to the territory of the unlived life.

Art of paddling whitewater or staunching blood.
How to guide a marionette, rub sticks for fire.
How to make one kiss matter.
The range of freedom. What the golden eagle might tell
about pursuit and betrayal.

The day foxes come from their dens
and salamanders from under their rocks.

Dream of rising from bed to fly alone through night cirrus,
greedy and heedless.

The fugitive pieces to the puzzle of the self.

The sexual jolt of the earthquake and its aftershocks.
How to decode other voices of the wild
whispering from marsh and river and sea.

All this relinquished, bargaining, bargaining,
bargaining again for ease instead of edge.

The Night Mind

There's a broken moon in the lake.
Craters tooth its inner curve,
and the movie has started to reel backwards.
Beach fires flare from coals to flame to log.
Chicken bones arc from the barrel
to the mouth and return firm-fleshed to a plate.
As we dive from iron-red water to springboard,
we're transformed from wet to dry.
Paddling in reverse to the dock, we grow
larger yet younger in every frame.
Atop the totem pole, a girl sits watching
nightwinds eddy pine needles from
the sand and restitch them to the trees.
Because time is ruptured, the girl's hair unbraids
and fingernails shrink. She dreams now
in many tenses. *I am. I was. I used to be . . .*
Words thin to syllables that fall
like glass beads from the belt she is unweaving,
and they mica the ground below.
Above, the flat cut-out sky presses down
until water fades to black, leaving
only the afterimage of a crazed moon.

Pantoum for a Member of the Wedding

It was the summer of fear. A jazz sadness quivered her nerves.
She was an unjoined person. A member of nothing.
The world, she said, *is certainly a sudden place.*
A green sick dream. I wish I was somebody else except me.

She was an unjoined person. A member of nothing.
Too tall for the arbor, she stared into a tangle of vines
A green sick dream. I wish I was somebody else except me.
Remembrances were sudden, each colored by its own season.

Too tall for the arbor, she stared into a tangle of vines
Sun-drunk bluejays screamed and murdered among themselves.
Remembrances were sudden, each colored by its own season.
But in the corner of her eye. Love. A thing not spoken.

Sun-drunk bluejays screamed and murdered among themselves.
The wedding was like a dream outside her power.
But in the corner of her eye. Love. A thing not spoken.
She was a wild girl. Strange words flowered in her throat.

The wedding was like a dream outside her power.
In blue light, she felt as a person drowning.
She was a wild girl. Strange words flowered in her throat.
She heard a chord then, a bell, an unfinished tune.

In blue light, she felt as a person drowning.
It was the summer of fear. A jazz sadness quivered her nerves.
She heard a chord then, a bell, an unfinished tune.
The world, she said, *is certainly a sudden place.*

The Lie of the Ordinary Life

A muster of white peacocks preens
by the inverted lake pooling the ceiling.
The peacocks are mute.

He is not quite mute. An inattention.
Letters answered in such haste, he fails
to answer. Words overlaid,
commas sliding out of line—a riff
of lost eyelashes punctuating nothing.

In this hungry place, there is a bed and a sign
noting the danger of temporary tattoos.

"I think," he tells her when they've fed one another
raspberries and champagne grapes,
"you may find me too ordinary."

An ivory plume breezes down, not yet knifed
into pen or dipped into black-squid ink.

His gift to her: a silver arrow lancing
an amber heart. And, of course,
the dense sweetness of his soap, his skin
on the pewter of her silky burn-out gown.
Her gift to him: a magic stone left behind.

Then the peacocks screech.
Gravity arrested, the plume begins to fall up
toward the mirage. Lake. Sky. A void.

Lunar Plexus

In magnetic air, my self or shadows of it,
the body a ballast for the head,
as I, smiling mask dragging an afghan body,
knit a new face from cosmic wool.

A three-dimensional life is formed by attitude.

You want what I have, so I must sheer
invisible sheep, comb and card
the fleece, twist the thread, ply needles,
then teach you how to do the same.

All done with mist and a mirror or two.

Still, don't expect to touch flesh. This wool
is thin, porous, soft but without affect
and, its anxious thread tugged by
an unseen hook, keeps on unravelling.

—after Leonora Carrington

Afterimages

Paint a picture with afterimages only with all the first colors
gone — only afterimages — and carry it so you have some
3rd and 4th afterimages. Study the aftercolors of any and all
objects and only paint the aftercolor.

—Ivan Albright

Doorbell corridor   rain-studded coat   face smooth
ears rough   neck arching   cheek-on-cheek   mouths   the weight of
morning   heat and smoke   tiger-time   clothes twisted   quilt
twisted   mango ripe   music   coffee   first the image   then luster
and refraction

and with the prime pigment gone   repaint   feel brush
beneath ribs again and again until *doorbell coat-damp* bristles lose
thrust   until a not-something is a scrim of something *knob twisted*
parquet patchwork quilt that happened then *Puccini* and again and
again to a person *rumpled shirt empty cup corridor mouth ripe* who
may have been you like

in the quilted field of Tuscan flowers   wine and song   ruby
figs   snake grass and wild oats now sepiaed with time *mango skin*
buttercup bed-spread bottleneck tongue and groove from bright
emerald to moss to celadon to patina *claret to peach to blush to milk*
to water muscle sleeked to bone *cheek-heat out-of-doors wild snake*
rough-smoke as color tints *parquet of morning* bleed into a faint
patchwork

a negative grace   image over image   multiplicity *viola nude descending lip-music   ripe oak and tannen   bent tiger bells* light-streaks through prisms *rain-smoke* landscape of then and now *morning-weight   arch   after-taste* subtlety of nuance *damp-twisted grass   aria* and the afterimage of afterimage of afterimage *hair-spreading quilt-rumple   door coffee spill* eye-echoes known *sheet-music* yet never again felt *coda* as story becomes vignette becomes moment becoming pause and

    hands   morning door to corridor   ears   patched breath cheeks coffee to buff   green to ripe   face-saving fig-flesh oat-spilling light   bright to dim then dimmer *rain-stripes* so shade *snake-smooth scent* so scumble and see it thin *butterfly tongue and mango-poppy   arch of smoke* until afterimages all merge *singers* the center pales *wing-shiver rain heat-spread lips brushing* then aftercolor washes at margins *the singing* objects *door the wild song* objectivity *the verse* rods and color-wands *the line bell the vibrato* straw and shadow matter *the rough silence*

Natural Defenses

I've never mastered the art
of protection

as a tree defends itself
against a giraffe
with bitter tannen that stops forage
and warns downwind
of danger. Or as a trout
hooked in a river
releases pheromones to alert
those swimming downstream.

Your reflexes, the fisherman warned,
slow down as you get older.

He was not speaking of fishing,
of course. But I,
disarmed by a taste for intensity,
less savvy than
trout or tree, forgot
to prepare myself for pain.
Even an old giraffe
remembers to browse upwind.

Violet, the Earthquake Girl

Pale and blue-white as her handsewn chemise,
she's wandered 100 years
amid urns in the Columbarium.
At night, the watchman glimpses thin arms and legs,
smells her unwashed hair, hears the rales
of her giddy child's breath.

She moves, he insists, in careless bursts of color,
veering from dark into light and back
again as she searches. When the walls
peel away, she walks through a forest
sweeping leaves with a twig broom.
As the path clears, she follows it,
sucking on damask plums
shaken from trees overhead. Her hands

are transparent in starlight,
feet, too, as she prowls, searching for
her home, for mother, father, brother, sister—
lost with the doorways, windows, china,
and mirrors and the seven times
seven times seven of broken, untended dreams.

Boxcar at the Holocaust Museum

Assaulted by brick and steel, my sister and I cross
the glass bridge between then and now, touch
Szumsk, the Polish town
our grandparents came from, walk into
Ejszyszki Tower eyeing photo doppelgängers
of relatives we call the monkey aunts,
of an uncle who couldn't skate the '36 Olympics,
of our parents, ourselves.

My younger sister has married a Baptist, raised
children who don't believe they are Jews;
yet she—riveted—is moving snail's-pace.
So when I come upon it, I am alone.
It's an old red cattle car like those from
our Missouri childhood, counted as they
clacked by full of livestock
due for slaughter. But this one is different.
To avoid passing through, I pretend to examine
oxidized razors, forks, tea strainers, then metal
instruments of torture which up-close
become umbrella frames. I check my watch,
consider flight . . . .

　　　　　　yet as I turn, I see my sister
by the boxcar unwilling to enter. *Why are
we here?* Hurrying toward her, I move past
cart, suitcases, hat boxes. *What will it tell us?*
For a moment, we are side by side, aware of
primal, physical comfort. Then together we step in.
It is dark. We do not speak. After 50 years,
stench still saturates the boards. As I inhale it,
I feel fingers tug at my pleated skirt,
at my sweater, my hands. Sweaty heads
I can't see butt me, begging for refuge,
those who would not have been spared:
my children, my sister's Mischling children,
my own Mischling grandchildren.

Suddenly, a soprano voice echoes around us.
Choo-choo. Turning, we see a boy-child
havened between parents.
He smiles, nods sweetly, beckoning to us and to
the invisible hordes pressed close. *Choo-choo,*
he repeats. *Choo-choo. All aboard . . . .*

Fugue State

She is in a fugue state. There are holes
in her arm made by the fat man with suitcase
and Uzzi.
As her husband, a red blossom spreading across
his chest, lies in her lap, she hears screams
and mewling. A swift—if imperfect—shield,
he'd wedged his body in front of hers.
Now while she cries, odd sounds
chirr from his throat.
She feels burning, numbness; and when she looks up,
tinted windows of his office
pewter the sky.
Somehow, he'd punched an outside line
so she could plead for help.
Now, though time creeps, they wait.
I'm dying, he manages, as cones from spotlights
sear, *and we need to say good-bye.*

This is only shock, she tells herself. Help
will come. Things will be all right.
We'll have children and beachcomb in Kauai.

Week-old tulips, ones she'd bought
for his birthday, gape in the crystal bowl
atop the desk. They are scarlet,

yet not as scarlet as the bouquet mantling his shirt.
Nothing again will ever be real, she murmurs.
I am beyond the rainbow.
Today is yesterday inside out. Tomorrow
is upside down. I was young, and now I am old,
because there are holes in him. In me, too:
both of us are leaking.
If there were holes in time, I would inch
backwards with him, babe in my arms,
seal them over, lullaby us into yesterday.
Or I would tell him how the wizard told the sultan
the earth is held up on the back of
a giant elephant, and the elephant stands on
the back of a giant turtle. After that,
of course, it's turtles—turtles, all the way down.

For them, the past was always overture. But now
his parched lips snap, turtle-like yet mute;
and past is everything, for she is in a fugue . . . .

Shadow of a Falling Bird

The shadow of a falling bird against a building
is more real than the bird.
Shadow of a glioblastoma on an MRI
is not real at all.

It may be short and brutal, the doctor says.

She sees the shadow of her own profile
on his shirt, sees a framed photo of
the shadow of a bi-plane across foothills
in the Valley of the Queens.

An approximation of truth,
only one measure of reality. She hears
the doctor's voice in the hard sanity
of morning, in the gray uncertainty of morning.

Monday is an Abstract Concept

Dog days of summer: Sirius rises at sunset,
sets at dawn. Old news, but her brain is unable
to track present tense. The glio is growing again,
forcing paperchains of days to unlink.
Now she sits for hours in the meadow
where Willa Cather wrote, watching honeybees,
listening to the *chuk-chuk* of chipmunks
and brush of redwings. Since she's lost numbers,
one to one-hundred scallop the air in random order
along with the black-white-gold predator above
who chills her with his nameless shadow.

August, no longer the eighth month, has become
an old college friend. She and August speak of
God and white magnolias. They read in the *Times*
how the crickets' chirp has been unchanged for
fifty-five million years. Though such fidelity amuses
her, when she turns to nudge August, it's midnight,
and she's alone. But cricket-song in the full moon meadow
coils around and makes her think of other old things:
how the gibbous moon brings a tidal bulge
and small moonquakes, how Venus—during
its night—looks not round but crescent-shaped.

Someone, her friend before August perhaps, has
asked about a lunch date for Monday. Or Thursday.
The days will not hold hands and stay in their circle.
Sunday is no where to be found and has, she believes,
run off with August. The remaining ones, those
open links, seem to have become colors instead of
placeholders for time. In the dark, their tones
iridesce. She will, she decides trumpeting a blade
of black grass, get someone to dial for her,
phone her friend to say they'll meet when it is
yellow and all the old, old, old crickets sing green.

Questions/Answers

What Is The Distance In Round Meters
Between The Sun And The Oranges?

She dreamed herself
into the Dickinson house
and put on Emily's clothes.
Shrouded in white cotton,
she meant to haunt Amherst,
inhaling time.
She wanted a soft song of restraint,
path of easy pain,
season without sun or oranges,

a sudden winter where
she could boot across cobblestone,
pause by a pond and watch
fish shadows in the shallows beneath ice.
Mindfulness rather than
unsifted chaos.

In a January thaw, she'd remember
how maidenhair uncurls in April
and hummingbird sips
nectar of a wild white azalea.
As Emily, she could spend
half-lit winter days
baking black cake
while she guessed how to reckon
distance or a life in round meters.

And What Was Beating In The Night?
Were They Planets Or Horseshoes?

As she lies wrapped in winter down,
she hears ghost horses gallop
the night sky. Then she sees them
with their comet tails
and manes of the Milky Way.

Come, they urge, touching her cheeks with
their velvety tongues. *We'll take you along.*

As she prays for silence,
the hoofbeats grow louder.
Other galaxies, new songs, they promise,
green cheese left behind
when the cow jumped the moon,
or white rivers where she might drink
and be drunk with joy.

*Faster than you can run, farther than
you have dreamed—a ride out of time.*

Her alien planet of a heart picks up
the beat, urging *yes* and *now,*
dismissing *why* and *maybe* and *what if,*
as it tries to break free of gravity,
and open its cool white cage of bone.

Does He Know That I Never Loved Him
And That He Never Loved Me?

1)

The man and woman are dark and light,
imperfect and moon-mad.
The light and dark faces of the moon
have different values, too,
yet both are cold under the Southern Cross.

Together, these two may see the moon
rise, but they'll never see it set.

He, with his short span of attention,
will look away first. While the round O
of the moon-mouth freezes her eye,
he'll wander off and
hallucinate this tale from his pen,

tattoo a wild white azalea
on her untouched breast,
put her astride a two-hump camel
and disguise her
with a hot cascade of blood-red hair.

2)

What she loved was who she was
when she was with him.
What he loved was the game,
himself pursuing her. For them,
a serpentless Eden in a sealed globe
where palm and sand and springs,
turtle and butterfly,
intermingle when inverted.

All that matters, he said, as he cradled the globe
till it opened by itself and a river flowed out
with whitecaps curled and pulsing
like those in a Hokusai print, *is artful matter.*

But the river could not be recalled.
Turtle was more than a shell,
butterfly more than a wing,
fruit was less than the tree,
and the globe had a price tag on it.
Sometimes when logic is lost,
agitation makes summer sand sting
like white-barbed flakes of snow.

Am I Allowed to Ask My Book
Whether It's True I wrote it?

It must have been someone else,
someone out-of-control.
This volume is elusive as carp
in a pond. I dip into it,
but past the shiny surface,
purple restlessness and broken borders,
always the dark surprise.
Secrets held close, like those
folded in pleats of a Japanese fan—

waterfall, bridge, forbidden tryst.
Or in petroglyphs. Does that one mean
sun or drought? Does the one below
mean cloud or storm?
And the lovers notched in stone,
are they moving together or apart?
Book, fan, petroglyph: each one
an old mystery to decode.

Carp skim with such idle beauty.
For an instant I see through
their fish eyes, but later
what I knew is only an echo of an echo.
Who was I at twenty? At forty?
Who wrote these words?
If we were reintroduced,
would I be face-to-face with
a friend or an unmeasured stranger?

The Color of Tomorrow

Chagall's lovers kiss in space. A blue cow nibbles sky.
Flowers teem in darkness beneath the earth
and ocean depths with foam-flecked horses.
It's January and plum trees blush
as the last persimmons rust on knobbed branches.

Yesterday's shadows are sweet on the tongue,
but how do we sample today? Can we drink the wind?
What if we wrap time in our arms and try
to inhale its wildness? Does a fruitful year weigh
more or less than a barren one?

Sometimes words are echoes of night-rain
and we sip their mystery, but sometimes they mantle
skies like aurora borealis with sheen
of the north and heat of the south. Is an hour
a decent portion? Can hunger be measured in days?

Like Chagall's lovers we kneel in cloud to drink
from the teats of the blue cow. How rich are
milk-tailed comets? What color is tomorrow
and how will it taste? we ask floating into canyons
of a thousand sunsets or welcoming the chrysalis

of dawn. Yes, you are beside me, but I am alone
measuring the distance to darkness.
I change direction once, again. I am still hungry.
How good is a promise? Have I dared enough?
Is that your hand holding mine? How long is now?

Contrariwise

Ruskin's Advice to Charles Dodgson

What we like determines what we are . . .
—John Ruskin

Flowers all. Crocus its head barely raised above ground.
Tulip nodding, soft skirt petaled on the hillside.
Lilac, a ruffled scent. You breathe it in
Before you see it.
Pansy and sweet alyssum, riot and pallor
Entwined in the shade.
Daffodil—early and bright yet quick to fade.
Never the rose or peony whose lushness fills summer
Nor waxen water lily, still life open to sun
And closed into darkness.
Trust the delicate bouquet of the woodland:
Buttercup, bluebell, meadow foam.
Don't ask them to grace your parlor or tea
Where they will droop and wither.
Blossoms should be left
Innocent in their beds, as nature intended,
For us to admire. Ever part of the wild undefended.

The Real Alice

It shall not touch with breath of bale
The pleasance of our fairy-tale.
—Lewis Carroll

All our secrets—even the birthday
and unbirthday gifts exposed in black-and-white.
In that book, he made me blond. Made me tall, then tiny—
made me feel slower than I was, made me feel
like *she* felt in the Wood Where Things Have No Names:
wondering who I was or how I got there and why I
had a bosom now and body hair and how old
I had to be before I could marry him.
Mr. Dodgson and I did play, though, where
I'd be Mama and tell him not to be late
and to wash the black stains off his hands.
Still, I called him Mister or Sir—and only
sometimes one of my pet names. You forget he had
sisters, knew about girls, and was twenty-six
when we first met. While Alice seemed to be me, he
was the White Knight, inventing, tripping, stammering.
So I took care of him.
But the best wasn't the stories or when he
made me laugh as I sat on his knee.
The best was standing on a wood box in the glow
of his darkroom. He said he loved the soap smell
in my hair, that I smelled girlish. But *I* loved how
the wicked smell of silver nitrate and colloidion
made me feel a little drunk
as we stood side by side watching the developing pan
shiver up its images of me. The eyes came in first.

Then the hair. Think about the Cheshire Cat appearing.
And we'd stand there, he and I, breathing synchronized.
He was always looking for the unplanned—
a curl, bare toes from beneath a gown, tip of a tongue.
And it was just us. There, holding chemical-stained hands
away from my body, he'd arm-hug me, give me
Eskimo kisses, talk to me as people only can in the dark.
But he was never improper.
Sometimes, as I was growing older,
as we stood touching elbows, he'd say he'd wait for me.
That was our fairy tale. Before he took something I
never got back. Afterwards, I was no longer just the Liddell's
middle daughter. Worst of all, I no longer knew where she—
that Alice—stopped and I began. I wanted myself back.
And I wanted him not to belong to the world. Then Mama
destroyed all his letters. So when you see the last
photograph he took, the one where I'm eighteen and
glowering, please understand I was struggling to remember
how it was before everything changed,
before we slipped from a land of wonder to Wonderland.

Beatrix Potter: On Children and Love

Now run along, and don't get into mischief.
—Mrs. Rabbit

My rabbits and mice, squirrels, cats, and ducks:
Bad mannered, sometimes ill-tempered.
Nervous or fierce creatures all.

A twitch of bunnies
A peck of hens
A snarl of foxes
A screech of mice
A scrabble of moles
A squeal of pigs
A pounce of kittens
A chatter of squirrels
A prickle of hedgehogs

And still, despite all, less bother than any child.
With my creatures, no spit or snot, screams or dreams,

No sass. No inconvenient incontinence or waste.

For he who would dare to love a human child:
A tangle of time and disarray,
A maze with shadowed paths of pain.

Wild Heart

I am the martyr. Just try the taking
instead of the sitting!
—Julia Margaret Cameron

Like Wordsworth I am always
looking for
Emotion recollected in tranquility
Not the literal truth but the truth
below
The truth
Quest or romance where
Any ordinary girl
Can be taken in the glass house
In each is my own filmy youth reborn
Idylls of sun-dusted flesh
Phases of the moon
Suggestive madonna
Daunting yet undaunted
All beauty arrested
Wild heart stilled one moment for us both

Xie: My Dear Multiplication Sign

My Whole's a victim I design
To photograph when days are fine.
—Charles Dodgson

Alice. I am so weary of hearing about Alice.
For all I care, she could have
stayed down the rabbit hole. I, too,
posed in the gypsy dress with one bud showing,
but on a chaise longue. And bare-limbed.
And don't called me "Z." Say "Ex-ey"; and it was,
of course, the X that made him call me
what he did. So you want to know if Mr. D.
touched me and if so where? Or if he kissed
me the same way he kissed Atty Owen.
Or if I posed naked like those bohemian
Hatch girls.

Or about Mother who
gave him my old clothes. Sewed collars
on them. (He liked us in outsize collars.)
For him, Mother bought children's stockings
in four sizes (dark so our legs wouldn't look gouty)
and found the acrobat costumes I refused
to wear. But I posed as a fur-trimmed Ophelia,
a boy, a poet named Penelope, two Millais oils
(*Asleep* turned out better than *Awake*),
and stood again and again with my violin.
The last time, at sixteen, in velvet. And I was
good at gazing into the camera.
The camera, not Mr. D., was the lover
I was too young to have.

Only hold still
for sixty seconds and stare, the way you
will into the eyes of the rich and handsome man
you wish to marry. Not allowed to
move or blink as Mr. D. rushed about
his photographic plates dripping and foul.
No smiles either—a smile
might make my face quiver. Violin bow
against the wall, so it wouldn't shake.
And I still haven't told you a thing? Well, Mother
wrote him letters, played his word games.
But you want to know about me?
Just look at the pictures.

(Beautiful, yes?
Those eyes! Especially the parasol picture
when I was sixteen.) I liked him, though
he was old, even more when Mother was
jealous. (She was.) And if you're asking
me about *Alice* again. If you want
to know *that*, ask Alice. She'll talk, tell
everything she knows. Though she's much
older than I, she doesn't know much.
Who cares about Alice?
And, besides, Mr. D. always said
that to get a truly stunning photograph:
"Take a lens and put Xie before it."

J.M. Looks for Alice in Neverland

Hook: Pan, who and what are thou?
Peter: I'm youth. I'm joy. I'm a little bird
that has broken out of the egg.
—J.M. Barrie

Girl little girl where are you
Mother little mother speak
Fearsome the pirates
Fickle the fairies
Slippery my shadow
How doth the little crocodile
How dense is the dark of the moon
How many miles to Babylon
Not Darling but Pleasance
Kitten or flamingo in her arms
Wild the weather
Fragile my heart
Chaste the looking glass
Who wants a button or kiss
Who wants to fly
Who will read me and take me to bed
Sweet girl who can't grow up
Alice little mother I'm here

Summer 1893: Little Lord Fauntleroy Meets Alice Liddell

> *I was a perfectly normal boy. I got myself*
> *just as damn dirty as the other boys.*
> —Vivian Burnett

Where are your curls? she asked. *And those velvet knee breeches?*

She, Alice, stout and with a dog-head umbrella. No magic here.
No poetry of thought. Thin lips, powdered smell of old woman.

You'll never live this down. Trust me. It'll follow you always.

The White Rabbit and Caterpillar lost. Tweedledee lost. too.
And no curious girl in pinafore eager to illuminate Wonderland.

Like that suit with the big collar. And you have a sissy name, too.

Together, I thought we'd enjoy an idyllic Mad Hatter's tea,
move around chair by chair, cup by cup, talking about our stolen lives.

An English Lord? she said. *Your voice twangs and your accent's horrid.*

Oh God, I'm drinking gin with a woman who criticizes everything
and barks like my old governess. Yes . . . Alice has *become* the Red Queen.

Why so quiet? Cat got your tongue? 'Twas your Dearest did this to you.

Too much growl and bite. So, suddenly, I begin to chase the Cheshire
Cat, desperate to fade from Alice's book and then from my own.

Alice in Storyville

I always spent every cent I got.
—E. J. Bellocq

Yes, I see my life through a lens. Insane, people call me,
or dwarfish. The Toulouse-Lautrec of N' Orleans.
Lies. I am and always was of normal size.
Storyville is my quarter, the working girls—
sweet Alices—I tip my hat to them
before I press their bodies onto my dark plates.
Unspoiled in their cribs, they like my manners,
diamond stickpins and red cravats.
And I, *mon dieu*, love their honeyed skin, sweet berries,
round limbs, and birds' nests down below.
What I want: to see through the looking glass.
What they want: a frieze of time,
colorless and without sound or smell or taste or pain.
Each in her photograph: a Mardi Gras queen, bare Rapunzel,
a child Magdalene with an aura but no orifices,
arrested before the ravage of time or disease.
I let them wear Mama's locket yet never touch them.
Spend my money on drink and fusions and ornaments,
so my degradation and theirs are tangential.
Only in my chambers—in a *ménage à moi*—do I
enjoy *les demoiselles*. Clutched in my right hand, a flat image
of a girl, pure and revirgined, while below
my sinister hand slowly fulfills its own unholy inclinations.

23rd Psalm of the Vivians

We shall slam them with our wings.
—Henry Darger

Eeny meeny miney mo my shepherd
Loves me loves not me
Boy girl boy girl
He is she is he wants she wants
There are green pastures here but I shall not want
Restoration
Take off my dress and put on the wings
This place may look like a pasture
But it's a battlefield
She was a little girl who had a little curl
Right up under her flowered dress
She was me unperturbed unrestored
So the girl says and Have it your way
She never looks down or back
A paper doll of a girl boy girl
A paper tiger of a boy girl boy
Curiouser and curiouser
The shadow of confusion she says is yours not mine
I shall fear no evil
I may tie a sash clip on barrettes
But I keep my sword under my dress
My rod and my staff they comfort me
Because I know where the bodies
Are buried and the curled-up secrets too
So I fear no evil
Goodness eeny meeny miney winged mercy mo
Boy girl boy girl girl
Love me or love me not Have it your way
This is not a sad psalm

His Baby Ballerinas

Ballet is woman.

—George Balanchine

because we are short of waist and long of leg
because we are elegant and thin
because we look like fresh-faced boys in tutus
because we sip water but swallow little food
we are so light we no longer bleed
we dance and dance and even in sleep we dance
dance through sadness and pain
dance to be the girl—yes, girl—Mr. B. loves most
our bodies bow to his commands and our demands
minds think only of elevation and *port de bras*
souls are slick now with sweat and rosin
our unconditional hearts are palmed by Mr. B.
our sisters eat chocolates and chips and have breasts
they run through fields with wind in their hair
they read books and have hours to waste
in the backseats of cars they drink Bud and kiss boys
but we bend and worship at the altar of Mr. B.
tired and tense and wary we have only volition
we are hungry and stunted except behind footlights
no longer his babies—now we are old children

Painter of Insecure Infantas

The best way not to fall back into childhood is never to have left it.
—Balthus

Legs liquid with light, knickers exposed, and beneath, the hairless sex.
Yet they gossip about me, Count Balthasar Klossowski de Rola,
when I am not the subject. Balthus is. He, paintbrush poised to catch

androgyny, that edge between innocence and perversity.
They ask about this, taunt and invade B's scant privacy, gape
at his girl-wife or the infantas—Thérèse and the others. But, look,

B can walk through walls, ghostly flesh, incubus, his boy-self
inhabiting the portrait girl's body, its awkward, wide-faced dream.
If she opens her eyes, his soul may fly out. If she exposes her hands,

they may trespass. Magic is loss or the *crac*; and B, a leap-year child,
born as Rilke said in the *crac* of February, can be forever
quartered in a world where both age and love are phantoms.

And where clothing is costume, except the slip framing the slit,
communion veil of intimacy—its lacy edge proof of reality. Mix
the metaphor and veil becomes white flag of surrender. Others call

this warped, fail to see *him* there in *her*. Her ecstasy, the revenant's
leap toward pleasure in flesh. Ask the girl warm in her chair with
puss in her lap. She could explain. Or ask the cat. *M. Chat*,

B himself, grinning as he laps at cream. He is also a child
under a spell, the anesthetized, the enchanted glazed by color.
Laced fingers atop the head tend an invisible brush. She/He.

As is the cat. As is the chair. The Alice who lies in the lap of the chair
shifts her position. Lucky chair. All girls are both found and lost.
All B portraits are of the self and layered in oil, in time,

in temperament. Not nymph or phantom. More doppelgänger.
Or equation. Foreground is to background, left is to right
as girl is to chair as paint is to veil upon veil. Peel it away.

X-ray it. See the black cartoon beneath the unfinished cusp-child.
Use sleight of hand. Now you see, now you don't. Girl? Chair? Cat?
Knickers? Cream? *Crac?* Balthus, insecure, unfinished child . . . me.

Selektion: The Painted Girl

*I'm interested in the stage of a human being where it's not so important
whether it's a male or female, before we can tell any social background or
anything, it's just . . . abstract, almost.*

                              —Gottfried Helnwein

like a negative bled dark   left too long   in searing light

it's blue   all blue   and the blurred child   walks amid

a street of bodies   her scant dress white   lips pursed

listening perhaps   to the blue flute   of a distant piper

the dead in coats and scarves   it's cold   but her feet

bare   arms held from her sides   and everything's blue

her head   injured head   gauze-wrapped   no face

blinded here   but is it worse   than the other place

where she knelt   wearing white panties   dark eyes

masked   by her own cupped hands   black-and-white

here   the only blues inside   where to go   what to do

but whose Alice is this   who will confess   piper

whose child   turned monochrome   how will she

bear up   pay   why must we select   our children

A Grave Lecture from Vladimir

The cradle rocks above an abyss . . .
-Vladimir Nabokov

Was it Shaw who once said the rumors of his death had been greatly exaggerated? Or Mark Twain? Does it matter? It was Shaw, I know, who said he liked children as well as flowers but didn't cut off their heads and put them in pots.

So while rumors of *my* death are *true*, yes, I still hover about here smacking my disembodied lips not over the human condition but over the prepossessing beauty of little butterflies. I didn't start it, of course. Even the girl baby learning to walk plays the vamp.

Don't blame me. I'm only the messenger. And what is the message? There's nothing like the butterfly—achingly female—with its promise of future sex. Remember how old M. Chevalier sang, "Thank heaven for little girls."

Thank *hell*, I say, if you've ever had to deal with them. Manipulative devils paving the way to the underworld = underwearworld with bad intentions. Why, actually, I never much liked real children.

What I most loved and hated and adored and suffered and desired (yet never pursued) was the glowing heat of woman pulsing through the seemingly innocent body of a luscious, juicy young girl. Boys run cold but girls run hot. And hotter.

Lolita? Who is she? Alice? Yes. Wendy? No. Eve—of course. Saint and whore, kitten and cat. Complain about me as an incorrigible, dirty old man. Single out the voyeurs as well as the perps (some gent = gender differences here).

But your bitching is abominably misplaced. We are lambs—all of us—(tho sometimes wolves in lambskin) led to the slaughter by Bo Peeps or Bo Peters (I'm bored now with the butterfly metaphor), tenders of Everyman's wet dream.

The Homelessness of Self

No Stork

Born on a windy day, I come down on the tail
of a dragon kite.

The twine is stiff and tangled, yet a few tugs
from my distant mother deliver me.

So cloud and rain and feral tornado: listen—
as does the dragon, the tortoise, the snake.

Know that curtains of morning and windows
of night open or close with or without me.

I am green as fields of corn, muddy as
our old river, whippy as cattails in the marsh.

Flight is my usual mode: flee from the porch swing,
from black and white, from home.

Under the radar, above the treeline, clouded,
I make and remake myself,

learning stealth from spider and wasp,
and from the queen bee, secrets of the hive.

Honey and sting—life-enhancers. Clouds with
little weight, the string cut, the sky open.

Forbidden Fire

Beyond violets and johnny-jump-ups,
Beyond the railroad ties:

A fort, a blanket, matches.
Like all secrets, a place of omission—

With a spring-wild pond for girls
Thin as April sap, lithe as snakes

Shedding skin. Girls' print dresses,
Slick with pond scum, dry on low bushes

As twig-fire warms bare white
Bodies, as beetles click, ravens cry.

But what of the man who crosses
The trestle, dark of face, foul of breath?

Aha, he says, *hotdog, hot damn, lookee.*
The girls freeze. *Tinkerbelles,*

He says, backing up, away. *Willis,*
Succubi, Vivian girls, Heeby-Jeebies.

Buccaneers of Buzz

In the old home movies a wild and giddy lot
The Pirates of Hillside Drive
The Stingers of Hampton Park
The Scourge of Richmond Heights
Flight is
When the flags and tulips shift in April wind
The whole swarm
In those degraded films
But amid the distorted colors
A dark body set apart
Crossing a branch or poised to fly
But looking for buzz
Notion of flight an ache behind the eyes
The girls are
The girls will
But I can't and won't
I will search for
Stun and sting
Gather honey and more
This addiction will be
Time can't
Films show me unwilling to alight
But there are others
See us
Outside the hive
We who know Emily
We who would be
Buccaneers of Buzz

Summer's Lease

I rise and fall, and time folds
Into a long moment . . .
　　　　—"Journey to the Interior," Theodore Roethke

As eagles scour winds of morning, cleat-clink
on the flagpole and a cell phone in the lake.

Not a day from the past, one of those
lost idylls with shovel and pail and whited
snail shells as we made sand cookies,
taught careless minnows to do the backstroke.

Still, watch out for the small girl on the dock.
In yellow-green water, you'll lose a dropped
fishing pole and spread-eagled child.

Below the mocking surface, who is she, who was she?

If we dig in the sand until water comes up, will her face,
your face, reflect from that shallow pool?

In Itasca where the mighty Mississippi begins to flow,
In Itasca, which isn't even Chippewa or Ojibway
but a scholar-coined word—
from Latin, no less, *veritas caput*: the true head.

Caput, the head, your head stores all myths
true or false, the Loch Ness of lies. Here, 2,552 miles
above the Gulf of Mexico, you drop a twig in the river.

A child wades, watches the twig, crosses the log bridge

between yesterday and today. Yesterday, you were
that child. See her, brown fawn of a girl, eager

to slip undetected among the cattails.
Shadow of wolf and coyote imprinted, shadow
of satiny skin time will warp and stretch.
Today you are the shadow in the shadow as

cumulous slowly bandages blue. Today's wind is
cold from the south. Today you told northbound
geese they were wrong-headed,

warned bear and turtle to think about shelter.

North is the way to winter. North, like *veritas*,
is the white within white.

Last year, your mother's friend died alone in
her cabin. Now her picture, in a boat-shaped
frame, sits on your mother's desk,
mother who, alone, still lives her arc of

a life, as do you, rounded, turning, puzzled,
deer tracks hard to follow in the shade.
Here, all ages are one yet are none.

White-capped surface of the lake is shook foil

in the sun, as the head of an eagle—who preens
on a branch above slapping water—dazzles.
No eagles when you were a girl, no fear of
the never-again. Only fear of what-if and ever.

O, song of the flagpole, sonata of wave and wind.
Out by the sandbar, in the shallows, wild
rice grows. Move toward it, wait, listen.

River or lake: watch twig and wing, take water
and light into your self. The lease is almost up.

Fly-Fishing for Sharks

Others count, but she sees
numbers and letters in gaudy patterns,
spends her days staring at the water,
her nights in the arms of a spiral galaxy
then savors the moment of waking and not knowing
who or where she is.
She wants to shed lines of the past,
feel scraped clean.
Sometimes safety is unbearable, she reminds
herself as she sees *Fly-Fishing For Sharks*
on the lower shelf
or a 7-inch barbed lure on the top shelf of
PawPaw's beach house,
promise left from a life no longer lived.
Her fortune cookie said not *A windfall,*
but: *There is time enough to take
a different path;* so she's fishing among
pools of letters and numbers,
trying to string them
into a message for tomorrow.

The Path to Innisfree

In some lost universe where Innisfree
had a rock with an iron handle,

before e. coli or giardia,
we knelt at the edge of streams,

cupped clear cold water in our hands
and drank to quench our thirst.

Then, lake isles were still safe havens
for the young and unmoored.

Then, we roasted stolen horse corn,
baked berry pies in a campfire oven.

We didn't know embers could grow cool,
or the waxed moon would wane.

How careless we've become yet careful.
We drink now from plastic bottles,

but have lost the path to Innisfree.
The moon is dark. The fire is out.

Disease and dis-ease. What we have
taken, must all be returned.

Beyond Blue

In the sky, look for the blue beyond blue.
    In the word, look for the sense beyond sense.

Open a shell and probe for a pearl.
    Find the thought in the seed of the thought.

In the sand, dig until water pools up.
    In the world, think backstory, understory.

Take the dead dragonfly and, one by one,
    Pinch off and save his gold-veined wings.

Sing of sky, seed, water, and wing.
    Sing what does not want to be said.

Sing the elusive song of the wandering
    And partly-redeemed self.

Painting with the Red Dot

Like a painting hung in some high-priced gallery,
he sees and knows one unequivocal fact.
Marked in red: she's taken.

He imagines her as one of Goya's naked
majas, unselfconscious on a red velvet chaise,

or a lush Cezanne still life. But she sees herself as
landscape by Signac or Seurat—in focus only
from afar—and otherwise, simply lights and shape,
a vagueness of multi-colored overlapping periods.

The period, after all, comes at the end of the sentence.

Her sentence, a life sentence. Being taken—oh multi-
plicity and simultaneity—symbolized by gold
bands and by the circle where she lives.

He proposes. She opposes. He, imagining some parallel
universe, sighs. She cries.

So . . . your life? Am I ruining it? she, an agitated
still life that won't stay still, asks. *Yes,* he answers
and then will not speak. Time has become
meaningless, elastic.

I have never been so lonely, he says, at last.

Love dispossessed. No fond gestures. No rambles.
No comfort of bodies entwined in sleep, so he
begins to pick at the dot. And she fears

this rawness—ultimate red—more than anything.
But still, he wants. He wants her real.

Currants, Currents, Undercurrents

Each day she permits herself only a green apple and a handful
    of currants which, with water, she tongues slowly one by one.
  Her sole work of art: her body. Slowly, for him, she sculpts it
        and the planes of her face.

      Crumbs on water swell into elusive white blossoms, vanishing
  bridal bouquet. As she treads to stay above the glazed surface, she
      watches mallards, webs sculling, circle her, creatures who
    mate for life. Any female—mate lost—must forever solo.

Falling water, I warn them both, *cannot be dammed.* Involved yet not,
    I watch their liquid dance of death. He cradles her head,
  and still the whirlpool sucks them in concentric circles, holds them
    breathless. At last, to save himself, he'll push off alone
and rise up from the river's rocked bottom,

        rise and fly a white dream plane past glaciers and a skull-
shaped cloud. Between peaks another cloud, in refracted light, a large
    cut-diamond. Above the polar cap, a ridged, uncanny moonscape.
  If a mountain splits open at midnight and no one sees it, does the cloud
    behind it become a question mark?

Her aqua solo was part of another life, that lost Hollywood
    rubber-flowers-on-the-cap one. Ballet in blue water
was trickier than on land. Never enough breath, an extension too hard,
  as she worried if anyone would ever love her enough. Moving water,
never the same place, hard to stay in place, her body then
  as always, as now—a traitor.

Any bottom, I know, is another false bottom—like those in
my green leather jewel box. Compartments inside compartments
        until, with the flick of a pin, one with a diamond springs open.
The would-be bride has no diamond, because love is hard, sex is,
                hard, and her hard eyes see past him, sees me, ring-
fingered, holding his life preserver.

The question she asks him is *when* not if. She still sees herself bridal—
        veil and ring—and whiteness everywhere. Though she longs
    to stand beside him in clouds of light, each time
                she reaches out, she pushes him away. And the currants,
    since she's so light she no longer eats, are strewn behind her.
                If sparrows peck them up, they'll be more nourishing,
        at least than bread crumbs.

        Her parents, who abandoned her, lurk behind a curtain
    while she struggles again to avoid being the dead girl.
            But her would-be groom wants her to be his wild river,
so she can open, eddy, and bend. *Don't drown*, she warns herself,
    afraid the baby's breath in her hair will unweave when she tries
    to remember the moves for her lean body and how to take it
            feet first into rapids then over the falls.

To on certain days, I'm almost willing to let her die.
            Or perhaps, without him, she'll eat more than currants,
    drink more than water. If not, I'll feed her pomegranate seeds,
        lead her down to the margin of the dark river.
            As she rehearses aquatic solos, I will
            show her lover a high path, beneath question-mark clouds
yet above the treacherous racing water.

Near Mis-

Harpy Curse for Mismatched Lovers

May the wild-eyed Calypso-girl turn aside and leave his life
Let her teeth and nails loosen and her hair grow brittle
May the threads of her voice fray and her shadow fade
When she tries again to steal his coin let him show empty pockets
Little thief swallows much poison but still grows stronger
Let us keen for this sister-woman yet give her new potions
Find her more hemlock and weed and datura
But bind him to the mast so he can't answer her cries
Weigh him down so he can't fly to her through the storm
Then let us beguile him with apples and honey and song

Virago Screed for a Missionary

Since his mother gave him candy instead of a switch
And his father never told him snap judgments snap back
If he takes the gospel of love door-to-door he'll get slammed
Help him to see his eros-tsunami is only a rogue wave
Let him learn to distinguish between pros and noes
And wherever he found this girl-woman he must put her back
Soon enough she'll want a leash and a muzzle on him too
He who follows the path of least resistance will have least
And any man who tries to walk on water will surely drown
May he see that being a caretaker applies first to himself

Chimera Cure for a Misplaced Heart

Make her burn the milagros and the copper witch's charm
Remind her he is Og the Leprechaun and Mack the Knife
Place her shoes pointing toward the door and paint it blue
Let us help her reckon the many thou-shalt-nots
Walk her through fields of riffling scarlet poppies
Whip her with his sly evasions and his dull silence
Show her once more his compass has no needle
Let us tell her again a wanderer will always wander
Then if she still craves danger she can join the circus
Even a wire without a net would be less dangerous

Banshee Rune for the Lord of Misrule

Let him kick his heels up like an ox without a bridle
But learn his wild strategies may need some tweaking
May he find Blind Man's Buff is no fun played alone
May we remind him all broken hearts mend with a scar
Tell him the dance of life is also a dance of death
Say a lie about a lie will sow lasting seeds of doubt
Say when milk is spilled the tears may well be his
And every arrow shot from a bow bruises the archer
We must urge him to value the picture more than the frame
May he learn there are universes other than his own

Beldame Rite for the Missing One

Let us remind her Tuesday's Child is not full of grace
So she can go outside and slash his name on a dying oak
Launder the shirt and pants that smell of his skin
Use his toothbrush to scrub the bathroom floor
We'll prompt her to try eye of newt and toe of frog
Say she mustn't wait for the phone to ring or shoe to drop
Tell her to plant foxglove and rue in his path
To give up useless celibacy in favor of promiscuity
When she throws darts at his portrait she should aim low
Then write an epic poem in which he does not appear

Gorgon Charm for a Mislaid Life

Remind him he can't mend Humpty or a broken woman
Tell him spending his days atop hot coals is inadvisable
Point out the holes in the gilded net tied over his head
Let us convince him the status quo is often only quo
That a half-empty glass will soon be drained
That a wandering minstrel is better than a whipping boy
If he takes the primrose path tell him not to pick wild flowers
Be sure his tea leaves show night and day with one who is the one
Let us help him find a new needle and a better map
May they lead him to fair weather and an incandescent moon

Another Blue House

– as if I had recently died and saw the house from a new angle
—Tomas Transtromer

Place of casual clutter—
High bed with convolvulus
Blooming beyond leaded glass.

A personal touch or a soft one.
Here every ghost needs an escort
And permission to leave.

No silks of mine hang in the closet,
No magic potions or creams.
Picture me a half-naked child.

Rice paper peels from the door,
The cat is fringing the curtains,
The locks have all been changed.

Released from the bungalow
And its dense field of gravity,
My shoes point due north.

Death is only a permission,
Escape works better in a novel.
Little bare ghost step lively.

Goldfish: A Diptych

—*Science has proven the goldfish
has a memory of a second and a half.*

Tale of the Goldfish

Look, there's a castle,
submerged so its world magnifies
in water hazed with algae,
but I see willow, sun, a dragonfly.

Look, a castle—
rays of sunlight through its doorway,
a mermaid on a rock
amid roots and burnished shells.

Look, there's a castle,
and I angle through the door, out the window,
everything static,
yet behind I sense a shadow.

Look—
its distorted world is pooling,
until I see a rock with no mermaid,
sense jaws of darkness.

Look, there's . . .

A Man is a Goldfish with Legs

Look, there's a castle,
where Circe turns seamen to swimming pigs
while the universe expands,
so watch out for solar glare.

Look, there's . . .
and at its hearth, a clockwise flame,
but below continents of ice,
stress lines.

Look, a castle—
and a pearl at my throat to keep me alive,
yet if there's heat lightning,
Venus will wink at daybreak.

Look—
how Circe takes up the pearl,
and Venus, in morning sun, floats fire and ice,
and may her lightning give you pause.

Some days—it's less than a second.

Homelessness of Self

All dreams lead back to the nightmare garden.*
—Janet Frame

In the airport, she sees women and men,
laminated identities swinging across their chests;
and the shop offers *fcuk*, a fragrance
with the line: *Scent to Bed*. The inversion
of letters is where it began or how, with one replaced,
saint became *slant*. Mother no longer tucked beside
Father into the dollhouse bed in the room with
a missing wall. No more clues. This murder was not
done with a candlestick in the dining room but
slowly, room by three-walled room, in a cheerful
round of miniature days lit by a triple A battery.

Is her biography fiction, people ask,
or her fiction biography? Not too different from
that sassy confessional poet who reportedly
writes ten minutes behind her life.

Once the doorbell rang. Once the window boxes
held flowers, and a porcelain cat crouched
in the front yard shrubs. But Goodwill has taken
much away, including Father in his quilted bed.
Today, a parade of seething nights,
dusty paths lead to a shrine of feathers, snake
and grass and silent claws. Now rooms here
have no light, and another wall has gone missing.
Time for the market cart,
green plastic bags, and a shit-stained blanket?
Do not attempt to reconstruct the truth.

If you think this is about drink or sex, you will be
both wrong and right. To orient yourself, trail
fingers of your left hand along the surface of
your two remaining walls. If you lose them,
the garden will grow, or you, like Alice, will shrink
until you can't reach high enough to smell
the reckless peonies or take the key waiting
atop the table. So what does it mean then to love
and be loved? Is it worth the risk?

The dollhouse was such a safe haven. Miniatures
may give the illusion of control, yet control has
vanished with the walls. She's left now with
feathered trails, highways, skylanes—lines of
uncertainty arrowing off in all directions.
She's lost because of sex. She's won because
of sex. She will drink to that, to an unsafe
snake-scented garden where she might wander
naked and unashamed. The slant is not quite
right, but she continues to plane it down.
The game, she insists, willing to discard batteries
yet not the candlestick, is riotous and disordered,
scent of bed in the air. But nightmare or not, it is
after all, worth each and every candle.

An Elegy for Lost Coin

Lost is when the trail frays to a deer path
or dust where footprints fade in August wind.

Maps can't chart the trail of a woman and man,
of a blue guitar and hot brandy, his song a tongue
never tracked, his coin unmarked.

This path is hard and rocky, the man once told
her. *Density can't be provoked.*

Shades of meaning are either found or forgotten
by a magpie mind, and bright bits of matter spin
like fireflies in a jar.

Yet fireflies spark less when the moon wanes,
tides are high then and low. So the boy

in the woods who follows a dog will be
lost near Almanor, and the girl who wants to
starve herself will keep on hiding the clues.

Or maybe lost is the arm-taped waitress,
the young one who tells her tale from table to

table at the Sand Dollar. Sister-daughter-roommate,
order the ribs, on Sunday no X-rays,
then the chiropractor made it worse. Tip her more,

her wrist is broken, but she can't call her father.
He's used her, so she's lost more than money,

lost trust, the nose stud, the aubergine hair,
the certain self—like the hungry girl
or the boy in the trees chasing a phantom dog.

Lost, like the dream I won't tell: how the man
with the blue guitar and I watch a dryer spin.

How we kiss while I try to nurse his child
who's failed to thrive, offering
a breast now soft and milkless as we pluck

an idle song. O, sing me, Cavalier, toast me
once again. Don't make me search for

firefly globes I pinched for jewels
or drag Almanor for the boy-child's pack,
for the girl, weightless as wind-sifted sand.

Though I've picked up old coin to pay the ferryman,

I'm not the waitress, not boy or girl but the woman,
and what I've lost must be spoken.

Trompe L'Oeil

Grapes to eat, a fresh-killed hare, bloodied
and dripping, white lilacs. Delft dish—
does a willow weep at its center,
the one that will not hold? All these things
placed by unseen hands—rifle propped,
blossoms strewn across butcher block;
yet the flowers have no scent, grapes no taste,
windmill or willow won't shift in the wind.

It was a day she thought she could hold and arrange.
Easier than peeling a grape or skinning a rabbit.
This day: hers to spend. Time would have
a taste, distance could be measured.
Slit the canvas and step into a darkened room.
Pull the curtain and throw the spread aside.
A place of no place,
here no dimensional colors glazed by time.

But this morning . . . the dish empty, fruit shivered
to raisins, the gun spent. No sun, no smile, no touch.
Time is stilled. Don't believe illusion.
There's no story. No picture—no eye nor I.

Stasis, He Says, Is Not the Object

Falling birds as white scraps of paper,
The mountain spiking a wreath of fog.

A promise, like a pomegranate,
Bleeds when it is cut,

This blood-letting more painful than most.
Each seed another bitter sweet. Don't

Count. Counting confuses the future.
Consider terror, yet don't wrap it

In the cotton wool of everyday.
Let the paper birds fly. Let the bloody seeds

Burst. Let the fog keep its secrets.
No matter what you do, he—discarding

Red fruit—will turn towards
Whiteness, step over the crest and vanish.

Why You Envy the Swallow

A swallow touches both sky and branch,
but his life is hard to piece

against the puzzle of yours. The scissor
of his wing flaunts

his freedom. The brush of his feather
recalls an old dream where doors

open and behind each one: anticipation
of an eager mouth, of a safe nest.

Apples Drop, Smooth, Cheeky

Mornings, the air zig-zag with
Striped wings, I kneel on the littered

Ground, seeking my gift
From the tree, just one unbruised.

Apple—yes, ever since Eve, a way past
The tree, past fruited plain

To snake eyes, then to the snake,
Chance to bite and be bitten.

Nights in the orchard, hoofs stir
Cider fumes as buck and doe

Mouth windfall. Then daylight again,
Heat, snake, a thrum of bees:

Coil of redness, of readiness, of a taste
For sting.

Scars

How the body marks time: jungle gym, tin can, cat
fang. Forehead, finger, leg . . . .

Physics: a scar is a way in and a way out.

Color her pink, purple, absent. Flesh can be livid
or torn yet will mend—like the ring between
her legs where the babies' heads crowned.

But other wounds are fresh, one the shape of
a wild white azalea. Little children—shallow scars.
Former children—deep ones. The azalea
gaped for most of a year, didn't want to heal,

until she seemed a Henry Moore: sculpture
with a hole anyone could peer through.

Through: a way to score, how to keep score.

Cheer for the underdog. No one likes a winner.
The more successful I am, the young star told her,
the more people seem to hate me. Welcome to the club.

Sometimes clubbed is how she feels, despite children,
spouse, books, house. But—wait—this rhyme
is accidental, accident of nature and nurture,
for surely *time is out of joint* here.

A scar is, after all, a joint of sorts, evidence of a life
lived, even if the joint has begun to crack.

Elemental physics: it's coming apart at the seems.

Yes, *seems* is what's intended here, for things are
seldom. *Seems, Madam* . . . And that's
why Schrödinger's cat can die before it dies.

But a scar is also a seam, part of the strip mine
of the body growing older, furrowing,
pitting—its beauty destroyed in pursuit of
the material.

She, like that star who finds himself unloved,
is guarded only by a thin, imperfect shield of skin.

The azalea: her mark of time, a little death flower,

small token beside the grave of her right breast.
Right breast, left heart. Heart left, oh yes . . .
left and left, that scar the invisible one,

as the hollowed chest seems to enlarge. Scar then
as a mark of absence: that which has been
lost in transition, the same way a woman of a certain
age becomes invisible. Only the hole stays

visible. So did Schrödinger ever consider the breast,
the heart? Can't they, too, die before they die?

House on the Mere

In morning light, the house on the mere
doubles, and she feels as if she lives underwater
in the mirrored reflection of a reflection.

If she says, *Come . . . my parlor . . .* she becomes
the spider or, in this waterworld, perhaps
the eel in the weir and her *other* still
prey. Her other: a troubador, a vagabond.

He wants a house, a home, a verse, a story

where he is not a man mirrored to infinity.
Though the glass may have been more than

half-full for the White Knight and Alice,
for this pair it's a world where drowning in glass
is possible and probable. The house

on the mere has a heron, a fox, a badger toying
with thoughts of liquid doppelgängers.
Each predator stuns with beauty, then tries to snatch
what he wants to feed a surprising hunger.

But below isn't a peaceable kingdom either.

It's a place where no one eats and illusion is all.
The table is only an idea, the bed a silky indifference.

It has an indentation of bodies but no presence,
unreal as her dream of cockroaches
where she tenderly rid the house of them,

carrying them out one by one in cupped fingers.
In waterworld, they have morphed into black
fry, which—to make him happy—
she seines from each airless room.

He, however, is the guest in this no-house-house,

in this home-never-home. Under here, where
they cannot eat or touch,

she's growing translucent and he's become
an Orpheus with lyre and rusting trident.
Seaweed curtains undulate, snails trace cursive

messages across sandy floors. Though she wants
this to be *their* place, he's weary
of holding his breath,
and the water weighs him down with grief.

These mirrors show everything yet nothing.

Fox, badger, and heron peer down from the shore
refusing to be doubled. But for him it's too late.

Here, the strings of his lyre have become restraints.
Here, the other is other.
He has lost his notes, forgotten his song.

Skin Is Often Rough

When the hourglass breaks, and sand trails,
summer is already old and steeped

at the horizon. Now the waterlily is gnat-seasoned
and wild rice reseeded in cattail shallows.

Happiness, I say, *is a careless word, dragonfly*
flicker between nymph and cooling air.

In phantom light, its outline
is faint in the wind.

Sand can be swept. A life can be threshed
but not replanted. Skin is often rough as the heart.

Each day, the grains tell a different story. Lighter,
darker, found yet diminished.

In Our Universe
These Things I Know Are True

as dusty scales on butterfly wings
       refuse to stick in a spider's web

       as egrets sprout fans of nuptial
plumes for the nesting season

as shadowy heartbeats alert
       a shark to the presence of fish

       so I in some alternate universe
will forever be curious yet true

Marriage License

Marriage is a cave with an underground river
and an unreliable torch.

The shadows on the wall are larger than I am.
Stalagmites, stalactites—all that liquid limestone,
seeping, dripping endlessly.

Pech Merle cave near Cabrerets, has
an ancient dotted horse and all around it
dotted handprints that say: *I was here*. At home,
my prints on the walls, doorjambs, a little SOS.

The best, though, is the cave of night, body
curved to body.

Warmth without stress, a knee wedged
between my thighs. Rolling, rolling on a white
sea—delicate ballet of midsummer's slight.

Animal comfort. Realm of the delicious unreal.
And don't forget the children. They don't forget.

Last night, dream-fragment, I lost my purse
in the lamp department of a store. Trace and retrace.
No purse. No honest man with a light.

Hello, Caveman. Was this money or only loss?

The man from Bolinas who came when I lost
power, who talked like James Earl Jones,
said he was there to help educate me,
that education wasn't as expensive as ignorance.

In a marriage, home maintenance is the daily mass.

Poet-philosopher-father from Bolinas has given
the sermon, reminding me to patch and hammer.
Still, a marriage is not a quilt or a work bench.

Hammer and mend. *Do you know any really good
marriages?* I asked my friend. *Jason and Pat,* he
said. *Morgan and Karen.* I'm sighing now.
The comfort zone: surf's up—don't rock the boat.

Monogamy, though unnatural has its points. Sharp.
Not alone, yet still unsafe.

Landmines. Walk carefully. The US government
wouldn't sign the treaty. But, listen—

a marriage is a minefield, too. Oh, god, drama-
queen overstatement, like people who use
the word holocaust for their small personal woes.
But the metaphor, as metaphor, still applies:

Watch where you put your feet. Don't look up.

Couples on the beach, old ones, always look down—
grays with Buddha bellies and matching parkas,
androgenous, pushing their metal detectors.

What will we talk about at dinner every night? we
asked at late night dorm talks
about LIFE. *How was your day? What did you do?*
The nitty without the gritty. Or only the gritty,

as I'm quizzed again about oil on the driveway, grass
growing between its cracks or a check written last year.

Check this: *hen-pecked* by its gender is something
a married woman does to a husband. No one discusses
the rooster who will peck at a hen's eyes and heart.

Is a heart a thing to be savored over time

Or just pecked slowly to death like in the peckless
marriage I once knew, before it turned feckless, before
the perfect old husband left my perfect old friend
for a young girl he met in a—yes—cocktail lounge?

And, dear reader, he married her. Pygmalion-like
(think 'enry 'iggans) he remade her. Cock-a-doodle do.

All I want is a cave somewhere. Think breaking
into joyous song. Now he phones his old wife to
talk tulips before mowing Eliza's grass.

But is the grass greener? Sometimes. Yes, the unmarried
can get up at night and read with the light on, fart,
don't have to pay for making someone
sit through *School for Scandal* one more time.

Once upon a time there was—scandal—a little girl
who had a single curl.

But she's no longer little, and this fall a writer
said she'd heard the erstwhile-girl,
cavegirl, had a lot of pepper in her.

Pepper? Is this another way to say *bitch*?

Marriage is the same jokes, same pepper and salt
in wounds, or as my father would have said:
the same old 66. And what was that? Even
Google doesn't know. Route 66, where I grew up?

Not as good as 69 but my father may not have
(oh, children and fathers) have known about that,
or if he did, he'd have thought I didn't.

So now past sleeping, pecking, aging,
and landmines, we've come up against the crux:

sex and money. Tax and spend. How much, how often.
Hold 'em or fold 'em. Fragile: this end up. If this
spree (insert money or sex) lasts more than four hours,
please call your physician.

To be a cynic on marriage is easier than finding a dipstick
to check the oil.

And marriage proves it's easy to be a math atheist. Here,
one and one should equal one but still equals two.
And don't take any wooden nickels or any license.

Tree frogs are singing now. Cave bats, too. No human follies.
They just want to be fruitful and multiply. No wounds.

In French, the word *blessé*—means not bless—but wound.

Fidelity is an insurance company, Eternity a perfume,
Infinity a car. Marriage is an insurance policy on eternity
and infinity. But sometimes both the days and nights
are too long. Sometimes the cave is empty. No prints.

But then there are the three words that put a Bandaid on
time and its wounds. Say those three words. Try.
And don't forget the children. Even if you've forgotten

why, the children haven't. They like dotted hands and caves
and still believe in forever, at least as it applies to you.

About the Author

Susan Terris is the author of six full-length books of poetry, 12 chapbooks, and three artists' books. Ms. Terris has won many awards for her poetry, including ones from the Poetry Society of America, *Florida Review, Inkwell, Many Mountains Moving, Missouri Review, Salt Hill, Spoon River Poetry Review*, the Pirate's Alley William Faulkner-William Wisdom Competition, and the Ann Stanford Competition. She had a poem from *FIELD* published in PUSHCART PRIZE XXXI.

For seven years, with CB Follett, she edited *RUNES, A Review Of Poetry*. She is now editor of *Spillway Magazine* (http://www.spillway.org) and a poetry editor for *Pedestal Magazine* and *In Posse Review*. In addition to writing & journal editing, she does freelance editing of book-length poetry manuscripts and teaches workshops on "The Making of a Chapbook." With CB Follett, she hosts a series of weekend workshops taught by poet David St. John. Ms. Terris has a prior career in the field of children's books where she had 21 books (mostly young adult fiction) published by Farrar, Straus, & Giroux, Macmillan, Scholastic, and Doubleday.

Ms. Terris was born in St. Louis, Missouri. She is a graduate of Wellesley College and has an MA in English Literature from San Francisco State University. She lives in San Francisco with her husband David.

Notes

p. 39 *"Women Lit/Unlit"* These poems are in the voices of or are about fictional women from literature. In the order in which they appear, they are: Tess of the d'Urbervilles (Thomas Hardy); Ophelia (Shakespeare); Hester Prynne (Nathaniel Hawthorne); Anna Karenina (Leo Tolstoy); Emma Bovary (Gustav Flaubert); Lena Grove (William Faulkner); and Molly Bloom (James Joyce).

p. 56 *"Kursk Good-Bye"* The poem is about the Russian submarine, the Kursk, which sank after an explosion in the Barents Sea in August of 2000. All 118 sailors died, but some died slowly enough to leave letters and poems behind.

p. 68 *"Fire Is Favorable"* The phrase "A stone, a leaf, a door" is from Thomas Wolfe's novel *Look Homeward Angel.*

p. 79 "Pantoum for a Member of the Wedding" The italicized lines here are from the novel *A Member of the Wedding* by Carson McCullers.

p. 81 "Lunar Plexus" This poem was inspired by Leonora Carrington's 1989 short story "My Flannel Knickers."

p. 92 *"Questions/Answers"* The titles in this sequence are from *The Book of Questions* by Pablo Neruda.

p. 121 *"Buccaneers of Buzz"* This is an Emily Dickinson phrase from the poem which begins: "Bees are Black, with Gilt Surcingles –"

p. 99 *CONTRARIWISE* This book is about the iconic image of Alice from *Alice in Wonderland*, written by Charles Dodgson, under his pen name of Lewis Carroll. The poems from this collection are all about men and women who had an obsessive interest in the lives of children.
Two of Charles Dodgson's favorite child photographic models were Alice Pleasance Liddell and Alexandra Kitchens – known as Xie.

The epigraphs here either identify the speaker or help define him or her. In the order in which they appear here, the poems are about: John Ruskin and Charles Dodgson; Alice Liddell; Beatrix Potter; Julia Margaret Cameron; Alexandra (Xie) Kitchens; J. M. Barrie; Vivian Burnett, son of Francis Hodgson Burnett; E. J. Belloq; Balthus; Gottfried Helnwein; and Vladimir Nabokov.

Acknowledgments

Many thanks to the following publications in which these poems appeared – sometimes with different titles or in slightly different versions:

Antioch Review, Ashland Poetry Press, Beloit Poetry Journal, Birmingham Poetry Review, Blackbird Online, Black Mountain Review, Black Rock & Sage, Blue Fifth Review, Blue Unicorn, Café Review, The Cape Rock, Climate Controlled, The Comstock Review, Connecticut Review, The Drunken Boat, 5 AM, FIELD, Flyway, Free Lunch, The Galley Sail Review, Great River Review, Green Hills Literary Lantern, Haight Ashbury Literary Journal, Highbeams, Hotel Amerika, Inkwell, The Iowa Review, Iowa Woman, The Journal, Kalliope, Long Islander, Lynx Eye Magazine, The MacGuffin, Many Mountains Moving, MARGIE, Marsh Hawk Review, New American Writing, New Works Review, Nerve Cowboy, Nimrod, Notre Dame Review, On the Page, Passages North, Ploughshares, Pedestal Magazine, Peregrine, PoetryBay, Poetry East, Poetry International, Poetry Magazine.com, Poetry Now, Poets On, Polyphony, Prairie Schooner, Pudding Magazine, Poetry Northwest, Quarterly West, Room of One's Own, RUNES A Review of Poetry, Salt Hill, Shenandoah, Skidrow Penthouse, Small Spiral Notebook, Spillway, Sow's Ear Poetry Review, Spoon River Poetry Review, Staple, Switched-On Gutenberg, Tea Party Magazine, Tertulia, Theodate, The Sun, Volt, Web Del Sol Review, Wind, The Worcester Review, WV (Writer's Voice)

Poems from this book appeared in the following anthologies:

Against Certainty, Poets for Peace Anthology (Chapiteau Press), editor, Ilya Kaminsky.

Claiming the Spirit Within, A Sourcebook of Women's Poetry (Beacon Press), editor, Marilyn Sewell

Cloud View Poets, An Anthology: Master Classes with David St. John (Arctos Press), editors, Morley Clark, Jane Downs, Susan Terris, & CB Follett

Collecting Life: Poets on Objects Known and Imagined (A Taos Press), editors, Madelyn Garner & Andrea L. Watson

Dorothy Parker's Elbow, Tattoos on Writers, Writers on Tattoos (Warner Books), editors, Kim Addonizio & Cheryl Dumesnil

Family Matters, Poems of Our Families (Bottom Dog Press), editors, Anne Smith & Larry Smith

In a Fine Frenzy, Poets Respond to Shakespeare (University of Iowa Press), editors, David Starkey & Paul J. Willis

Nice Jewish Girls, Growing Up in America (Plume/Penguin*)*, editor, Marlene Adler Marks

Pushcart Prize XXXI, Best of the Small Presses, editor, Bill Henderson, Pushcart Press, for "Goldfish"

So Luminous the Wildflowers (Tebot Bach), editor, Paul Suntup

When She Named Fire, An Anthology of Contemporary Poetry by American Women (Autumn House Press), editor, Andrea Hollander Budy

Words and Quilts (The Quilt Digest Press), editor Felicia Mitchell

Prize-winning poems from this book:

"Afterimages"; "Boxcar at the Holocaust Museum"; "Currants, Currents, Undercurrents"; "Eye of the Water Lily"; "Goldfish"; "Lunar Plexus"; "Mary Todd Lincoln at Ford's Theatre"; "Molly Has the Last Word"; "Painter of Insecure Infantas"; "The Real Alice"; "Xie: My Dear Multiplication Sign"

Several of the poems from *The Homelessness of Self* were first published in *Marriage License*, which won the 2007 Pavement Saw Chapbook Award

Titles from Marsh Hawk Press

Jane Augustine, *A Woman's Guide to Mountain Climbing,*
Night Lights, Arbor Vitae

Sigman Byrd, *Under the Wanderer's Star*

Patricia Carlin, *Quantum Jitters, Original Green*

Claudia Carlson, *The Elephant House*

Meredith Cole, *Miniatures*

Neil de la Flor, *Almost Dorothy*

Chard deNiord, *Sharp Golden Thorn*

Sharon Dolin, *Serious Pink*

Steve Fellner, *The Weary World Rejoices, Blind Date with Cavafy*

Thomas Fink, *Peace Conference, Clarity and Other Poems,*
After Taxes, Gossip: A Book of Poems

Norman Finkelstein, *Inside the Ghost Factory, Passing Over*

Edward Foster, *Dire Straits,The Beginning of Sorrows, What He Ought To Know,*
Mahrem: Things Men Should Do for Men

Paolo Javier, *The Feeling Is Actual*

Burt Kimmelman, *Somehow*

Burt Kimmelman and Fred Caruso, *The Pond at Cape May Point*

Basil King, *77 Beasts: Basil King's Bestiary, Mirage*

Martha King, *Imperfect Fit*

Phillip Lopate, *At the End of the Day: Selected Poems and An Introductory Essay*

Mary Mackey, *Sugar Zone, Breaking the Fever*

Sandy McIntosh, *Cemetery Chess: Selected and New Poems,*
Ernesta, in the Style of the Flamenco, Forty-Nine Guaranteed Ways to Escape
Death, The After-Death History of My Mother, Between Earth and Sky

Stephen Paul Miller, *There's Only One God and You're Not It, Fort Dad,*
The Bee Flies in May, Skinny Eighth Avenue

Daniel Morris, *If Not for the Courage, Bryce Passage*

Sharon Olinka, *The Good City*

Justin Petropoulos, *Eminent Domain*

Paul Pines, *Last Call at the Tin Palace, Divine Madness*

Jacquelyn Pope, *Watermark*

Karin Randolph, *Either She Was*

Rochelle Ratner, *Ben Casey Days, Balancing Acts, House and Home*

Michael Rerick, *In Ways Impossible to Fold*

Corrine Robins, *Facing It: New and Selected Poems, Today's Menu, One Thousand Years*

Eileen R. Tabios, *The Thorn Rosary: Selected Prose Poems and New (1998-2010), The Light Sang As It Left Your Eyes: Our Autobiography, I Take Thee, English, for My Beloved, Reproductions of the Empty Flagpole*

Eileen R. Tabios and j/j hastain, *the relational elations of ORPHANED ALGEBRA*

Susan Terris, *Ghost of Yesterday, Natural Defenses*

Madeline Tiger, *Birds of Sorrow and Joy*

Harriet Zinnes, *Weather Is Whether, Light Light or the Curvature of the Earth, Whither Nonstopping, Drawing on the Wall*

Artistic Advisory Board
Toi Derricotte, Denise Duhamel, Marilyn Hacker,
Allan Kornblum, Maria Mazzioti Gillan, Alicia Ostriker, Marie Ponsot,
David Shapiro, Nathaniel Tarn, Anne Waldman, and John Yau.

For more information, please go to: http://www.marshhawkpress.org.